CODE NOIR

CODE NOIR

AFRO-CARIBBEAN STORIES AND RECIPES BY LELANI LEWIS

T tra.publishing

FOREWORD

Code Noir is a cookbook steeped in history. Not only because of its title, which references a seventeenth-century decree by Louis XIV outlining how enslaved Africans in the French colonies were to be treated (see p. 12), but primarily because it delves into the food and the people who, due to the horrific course of history, came together in the Caribbean, bringing ingredients from the Old World and the New World onto a single plate.

In this book, you'll find stories about those ingredients, their journeys, and their role in the everyday meals of people from the Caribbean. I know few people who read a cookbook from start to finish—I myself am guilty of this: I usually flip straight to the enticing recipe photos—but *Code Noir* wishes to engage you as much with the stories behind the dishes as with the hunger-inducing images and recipes. Hopefully, you find them as fascinating as I do.

It's important to note that "Caribbean cuisine" does not exist as a singular entity—understandably, considering the area spans many thousands of miles and consists of more than a thousand islands. The Caribbean is often divided into the Greater and Lesser Antilles. The Greater includes four islands: Cuba, Jamaica, Hispaniola (with Haiti and the Dominican Republic), and Puerto Rico. The Lesser, which can be subdivided into the Windward and Leeward islands, lies more to the southeast and consists of thirteen countries, including islands such as Bonaire and Curaçao, Saba, Sint Eustatius, and Sint Maarten. There, you'll find more than thirteen ethnic groups and many languages from which new Creole languages have emerged. In addition, countries bordering the region are closely tied to the area, partly through CARICOM, an intergovernmental organization that promotes economic integration and cooperation. In addition to the Caribbean islands, Suriname, Belize, and Guyana are members of CARICOM.

There is no island in the Caribbean that hasn't been tossed back and forth like a marble on a schoolyard between the colonial hands of the Spanish, English, French, and Dutch. These European powers rejected and alienated centuries-old cultures, agriculture, and technology. They forced their language, religion, and food into the culture and brought people from all over the world to this region.

Despite the significant diversity, there are many similarities among the countries, not only in flora and fauna but also in the nature of the inhabitants, even with their varied backgrounds, yet it's impossible to pinpoint one dish that could typify the entire region. When I refer to Caribbean cuisine, I refer to the food of the whole area, and I will always clarify which country I'm specifically discussing.

When I began to delve into the history of Caribbean kitchens a few years ago, I realized that so many ingredients that we use daily around the world in various ways have intriguing and complicated histories and origins. This insight led me to a philosophy I want to be reflected in my work: the idea that food is a tangible way to bring people of all backgrounds together, regardless of perceived differences. A quote that perfectly encapsulates this is:

"With a deeper understanding of the movement of these ingredients, we'll see just how connected the whole world is by the food that we consume."
– Chris Ying in *You and I Eat the Same* (2018)

I invite you to browse through the photos, prepare recipes you could not even have dreamed of, and tantalize your taste buds with new combinations of spices. I hope you learn something from this book, perhaps even about yourself, but most importantly, I hope you enjoy it.

Lelani Lewis

A MONSTROUS DOCUMENT

Food is a fundamental aspect of our lives, nourishing not only our bodies but also our minds and souls. Shared meals can connect and liberate us, yet food can also be used as a means of oppression. A horrific example of this is the era of slavery.

From 1550 to 1800, millions of African men, women, and children were kidnapped, enslaved, and transported across the Atlantic Ocean. Some Africans fled from to the interior of the continent to the coast to escape tribal wars—funded and armed by Europeans—only to end up captured. The conflicts were so frequent that women started to conceal seeds in their hair, in perfectly plaited cornrows to ensure they had sustenance in case they too were kidnapped. This is how fruits like ackee arrived in the Caribbean.

On slave ships, familiar food was used to calm and placate the enslaved. Similarly, on plantations, they were provided just enough sustenance to labor, but not enough to muster the energy to revolt. Food, thus, was used as a tool for suppression.

The amount they were fed was even codified in law. The name of my book, *Code Noir*, is derived from these French regulations. This decree, enacted by Louis XIV in 1685, remained in effect until 1848. It dictated the treatment of enslaved Africans, particularly in the French colonies like the French Antilles and what is now Louisiana in the United States, with a primary focus on slavery within sugar plantations. This document is known as one of the most monstrous legal texts of modern times as it detailed how enslaved Africans were to be controlled, fed, punished, and who had "rights" to their ownership. It vividly portrays the dehumanization of Africans.

The document's initial stipulation demanded the expulsion of all Jews from the French colonies—a policy in alignment with the one in France. The second point was that everyone in the colonies, including enslaved Africans, had to reject their religions and convert to Catholicism. The fifty-eight other articles in the *Code Noir* detailed how to treat enslaved Africans. Here are some examples:

Article XII. Children of married slaves are born as slaves. If the man and woman have different masters, then the child is the property of the mother's master, not the father's.

Article XVI. It is forbidden for slaves from different owners to assemble, neither during the day nor at night, not for a wedding nor any other excuse, not in the master's house nor elsewhere. They risk physical punishments, no lighter than the whip or branding, and for repeat offenders and in other aggravating circumstances, they can be punished with death, a decision that is up to the judge.

Article XXXVIII. Of a slave who has been on the run for a month, the ears are cut off, and he is branded with a fleur-de-lys on the shoulder. If he remains absent for another month, his Achilles tendon is cut, and he is branded again. If the slave was to run away for a third time, he would be executed.

The mere existence of such a document is horrifying, and the chilling fact that it was strictly adhered to for nearly two centuries is deeply unsettling. It is appalling that the laws of the time subjected one person's free will to that of another. And to think that this was considered a reasonable and fair way to treat enslaved Africans. One of the articles in the *Code Noir* stipulated that a mother, father, and child should not be separated. Regrettably, this was not always adhered to. Despite the passage of time, the visible scars of separated families linger on.

So, why would I name this book after such a repugnant document? We should always scrutinize history with a critical eye, as it is often written by the victors, or the 'hunters' glorifyng their spoils, but the other side of the story also needs illumination. Let us learn from past mistakes. Let's reclaim and invert the term from the lingering trauma caused by the trans-Atlantic slave trade to a narrative about the pride and innovations of those who made a home in a new place. Under the most appalling circumstances, with limited resources and time, the enslaved were able to create fantastic dishes that seeped into the cultures not only of the Caribbean but of many countries in the Americas, where they even became national dishes at times. Like feijoada in Brazil, saltfish and ackee in Jamaica, and pepperpot in Guyana. This is the *Code Noir* I now present to you.

FAMILY AND IDENTITY

Growing up in South London, I was the product of a mixed marriage: my mother was Irish (a "plastic paddy," an Irish person born in Britain), and my father hailed from Grenada, one of the Windward Islands of the Lesser Antilles. This blend of cultures within the melting pot of London contributed to a wealth of cuisines and ingredients at our dinner table. We had relatives and friends from all corners of the world. They, and the dishes they brought with them, invariably formed a colorful and diverse mix in our house. We ate Caribbean, Indian, Pakistani, Mauritian, Italian, Irish, and everything in between. All bursting with flavor, peppers, herbs, and spices. My godmother would fry eggplant until crispy in chickpea flour in the Mauritian style. We had warming Irish stews with suet dumplings. Pakistani friends served curry and taught my parents how to properly cook basmati rice, complete with sweet, caramelized onions.

Unlike most families at the time, my father was the chef at home. My mother learned to cook from him; she could barely boil an egg when they first met. My father's sisters were also on hand from the beginning to guide my mother, "this woman," in the kitchen. They taught her the recipes for roti and curry, and of course rice and peas. Thus, my mother underwent her rite of passage into Caribbean food culture—and I experienced my own alongside her. For special occasions, we made dahl puri roti, an unleavened bread with ground split peas in the dough. It is still my favorite. We spent hours kneading, filling, rolling, and frying. Ironically, it was my Irish mother who taught me to make these Indian flatbreads, a skill she acquired through her exposure to Caribbean cuisine.

Although my mother's culinary career had a bumpy start, our house became the go-to place for holidays and parties—and that meant lots of food. Birthdays, christenings, first communions: they revolved not so much around the religious ceremony, but primarily served as an excuse to eat together. My parents would clean the house for days beforehand, drive to Billingsgate or Smithfields (wholesale markets for restaurants where you could get the best cuts of meat and freshest fish) at five in the morning, and spend hours in the kitchen.

FAMILY COOKOUT AT GRAND ANSE BEACH, GRENADA

AS A CHILD TRAVELING WITH MY AUNT, MOTHER, AND COUSIN TO CARIB'S LEAP, GRAND BRAS RIVER (GRENADA), AND CARRIACOU.

The preparation might have been laborious, but the result was always a delightful spread of dishes on our buffet tables. With roti and a curry dish—boneless, as my mother preferred it—fried chicken, rice and peas, saltfish souse, stewed peas, coleslaw, potato salad, fried plantains, and fried fish or a whole roasted salmon. It sounds like a lot, and it was. My father had eleven brothers and sisters and a host of cousins, nieces and nephews, and great-aunts and great-uncles. Yet there were always leftovers: the entire family knew that when they went to Conrad and Sandra's, they should pack a load of Tupperwares to take home leftovers.

There was an abundance of food and drinks, with soca or lovers' rock music blaring from the speakers, while my Aunties taught us how to sway our hips to the rhythm of one of my favorite songs: "cent, five cent, ten cent, dollar." That was the Caribbean side. On the contrary, the other, Irish side of the family though not as vivacious, still had a quiet charm and warm hospitality. I was lucky enough to grow up near my maternal grandparents and often stayed with them. It was a highlight, as my Gran spoiled her grandchildren terribly.

My grandparents belonged to the generation with a strict traditional role division. Although they both worked, I don't know if my grandfather knew how to turn on the gas stove, let alone cook a meal. Well, that's not entirely true, because there was one thing he mastered: steak with fried onions, boiled potatoes, and peas, served with brown sauce. I remember not being very interested in my own plate, but always took bites from my grandfather's, which tasted better. I don't know if it was because he mashed his potatoes, peas, and onions, or the way he always cheerfully tapped his foot on the floor when taking a bite.

My Gran would diligently make dinner from scratch every night for my Grandad, who would always without fail complain about it. Everything was homemade: you would never find anything ready-made in her kitchen. The fare was hearty, unfussy and rich in potatoes: you might have stews with beef and suet dumplings, one night or boiled potatoes, with ham and cabbage, the meat and two veg trifecta common to this generation. Beef stew with suet dumplings, or potatoes with ham and cabbage—always potatoes, meat, and vegetables, as was customary for their generation. But sometimes Gran felt adventurous, then she

A PHOTO I CHERISH: MY LARGE AND DIVERSE FAMILY

made curry from a jar with raisins (the only exception to the no ready-made rule) and egg salad with salad cream (a type of sweet and sour mayonnaise). And if I was lucky—and I always was with Gran—I got a dessert: a Cornetto, jelly (Jello), ice cream with fruit, or cake with custard. It might not have been very exciting food, but it was nourishing, both for the body and for the soul.

One of the most prominent characteristics of my Gran was her warm and generous hospitality. You could never go to my gran's house and come away unfed or watered with mugs of tea, I felt sorry for anyone who might refuse a cup of tea. If she only had dinner for two and an unexpected visitor, you'd be damned if she didn't make it stretch three ways. The stereotype of the Irish insisting on pushing food onto you held true for my Gran. In my adolescent years, filled with insecurities about my body, whenever I visited her, she never failed to insist that I have a slice of cake with my tea. "No" wasn't an answer she'd accept. "You're getting too thin," she would insist.

The generosity from both sides of my family was contagious. From a young age, I observed how food could transform human interactions; how a simple gesture of offering food could elicit the warmest of smiles. After years of exploring various careers, it made perfect sense that my final destination revolved around food—an integral element of my life.

Growing up in South London, my childhood was significantly shaped by the local Caribbean community, which had settled there in the post-war period. From the late 1940s to the 1970s, the United Kingdom had urged residents of the British Commonwealth to migrate to the "motherland" to address the labor shortage. Many residents of the British colonies in the Caribbean heeded the call and relocated, mostly to London: the Windrush generation. They often chose to reside near acquaintances, and popular neighborhoods were Notting Hill and Brixton. I lived in Streatham, not far from Brixton, where my father would take us every Saturday to the bustling market stalls on Electric Avenue to stock up on Caribbean ingredients. Vendors, with their Cockney-accented calls of "3 plant'in for a pound," lured us in. Besides the vibrant fruit and vegetable stalls, there were Turkish butchers, hair shops, and Caribbean bakeries, where we'd buy a snack while shopping.

The customer service in Caribbean eateries was as sparse as the array of food available for purchase. I found it intimidating to step inside, let alone to order food. I usually encountered someone with a stern expression, demanding "wha ya want?" After bravely suggesting an item, I'd be met with a curt "me, not have dat." The back and forth continued until I finally suggested something they had in stock. However, the food was so delightful that I would endure the whole drama again without hesitation.

Much of my life and experience with Caribbean food and people unfolded in this Caribbean diaspora in London; I only visited the Caribbean a few times. Therefore, my experience with Caribbean food culture is not confined to one island or area but spans a whole range. I grew up eating Trinidadian and Guyanese roti—reputedly among the best— Jamaican saltfish and ackee, Haitian pikliz, Grenadian oil down, cou-cou, and flying fish from Barbados. London predominantly features food from former British-colonized islands, and that is the cuisine I know best. Consequently, this book mainly offers recipes from these regions. Having been raised in London, I am also familiar with the many substitutes that people used to come as close as possible to the genuine taste of home, as not all the original ingredients were available in the United Kingdom.

One of the beautiful aspects of growing up in the Caribbean diaspora is that it provided me with a broader perspective, sparking an insatiable curiosity not only about my father's homeland but also about the cuisines of other islands and how they compare or contrast. This curiosity eventually led to extensive research into Caribbean food culture, culminating in the creation of my platform,

Code Noir, in 2020 (see p. 24). I had a deep desire to understand the origins of various dishes, and how the centuries-long ebb and flow of diverse groups of people and cultures have shaped these delightful and varied cuisines.

Food research also served as a means to reconcile with my own identity. In a society where everyone is constantly put into boxes, being a woman of mixed ethnic origin is often complex. Food became my conduit to connect my seemingly disparate backgrounds. It's not unusual for people of mixed ethnicities to feel like outsiders, perpetually on the fringe of any group. We're often told that we aren't sufficiently one thing—be it Caribbean or Irish—to authentically claim either identity. I'll never forget the time when, after sharing with a friend my involvement in a movement advocating for increased representation of BIPOC (Black, Indigenous, People of Color) in the culinary world, he responded, "But you're not black!" His comment shocked me, it hurt. I had not experienced the white privileges my mother did. Food became my solace.

By solace, I don't mean indulging in tubs of Ben & Jerry's. Rather, I actively began to seek connections between the cultures that make up who I am. And what did I find? Irish and Caribbean cultures indeed share common ground. During the time of the Windrush generation, Caribbean workers migrating to the United Kingdom were hardly welcomed. Signs in pubs read "No Irish, No Blacks, No Dogs." Irish and Caribbean people seemed to have nothing in common, but now, discrimination seemed to bind the two groups together.

This connection became more evident to me a few summers ago while I was teaching in Amsterdam a course on Caribbean culinary history. It was an interactive workshop where students were tasked with designing eating rituals, evoking significant food memories, and creating a Caribbean cocktail. They chose Guinness punch—a cherished drink across several British-colonized islands, composed of a potent blend of stout beer, creamy, sweet condensed milk, and a sprinkle of cinnamon and nutmeg. Guinness is known to me through both sides of my family. I understood the Irish connection, Guinness having been founded in Dublin, but why did I also know it from the Caribbean side? I investigated and discovered that the Irish were appointed as indentured laborers on plantations in the Caribbean in the seventeenth century. Due to their significant presence in the region, Guinness decided to export its beer there, fortified with more alcohol and hops to withstand the Atlantic journey. It gave me a sense of solidarity, knowing that these two cultures are tangibly linked through food.

MY GRANDMOTHER AND AUNTS. THE BOY
ON MY GRANDMOTHER'S LAP IS MY FATHER.

My desire to cook Caribbean food grew stronger when I moved to Amsterdam. I missed home, I missed my family, and I frequently sought comfort in Asian and tropical supermarkets where I found ingredients that were the same or similar to those at home, albeit under different names—names brought to Amsterdam by the Surinamese community. I enjoyed seeing these parallels, but the food I tasted here was not the same as the Caribbean food I craved. So, I started making it myself. And not just for me. I hosted my first pop-up at a Caribbean bar, Rum Barrel on Javastraat, with a supposedly "easy" (oh, the irony) eight-course dinner. I remember starting with not an ounce of experience, and how exhausting the work was—from preparation to decoration and marketing—especially while juggling my full-time job. However, I found the experience addicting, leading me to host pop-ups all across Amsterdam. I noticed that few people knew much about Caribbean cuisine beyond jerk chicken. I wanted to teach them more, but to do that, I had to broaden my own knowledge. This marked the beginning of thorough research, a quest I'm still on. The result of this self-education was *Code Noir*.

At first glance, *Code Noir* is an interactive dinner where we explore the culinary history of the Caribbean. But for me, it signifies so much more. It embodies the notion that food unifies rather than divides. Many of the migrants who came to the Caribbean—whether by force or choice—carried with them something familiar and edible. Europeans brought grains and livestock; Africans brought plantains, black-eyed peas, nuts, and fruits. The Chinese introduced noodles and bok choy, and the Indians brought roti, turmeric, and much more. The fusion of these ingredients and techniques birthed the melting pot cuisine of the Caribbean. Even though roti originates from India, over time, people stopped associating it with just one place. Roti became part of the cultural identity of the Caribbean— and for the Dutch, a part of Surinamese culinary culture— just as Peruvian potatoes became a key ingredient in the Dutch national dish: stamppot. This illustrates that however we perceive national identity and culture, all boundaries melt away through the food we consume. And that is the essence of this book: we are all interconnected by what we eat.

PICKING FRESH MANGOS WITH MY PARENTS IN MY AUNT MARIE-CLAIRE'S GARDEN.

CODE NOIR

"Until the lions have their own historians, the hunt will always be glorified by the hunters." —Chinua Achebe

Code Noir began as an exploration of my identity and dual heritage: my quest to comprehend and reconcile the cultural mélange I represent, with a Grenadian father and an Irish mother, and growing up in London. Seven years ago, I had just relocated from London to Amsterdam and was craving the comfort food of home: Caribbean cuisine. Food, a crucial part of my family and personal life, became the central theme of my journey to self-discovery.

After organizing various pop-up restaurants in Amsterdam, I realized that there were more questions than answers about Caribbean food. People feared it would all be spicy, or they only knew of jerk chicken. This ignorance frustrated me, but my own lack of knowledge frustrated me even more. So I began to search, read, cook, and listen. The cuisine and culture of one half of my heritage enthralled me, and I felt an urgent need to know more. This journey allowed me to interconnect the seemingly disparate cultures within me. Along the way, I discovered that the Caribbean's culinary culture itself is an enormous melting pot, drawing from cultures across five continents.

During my research, I read about a seventeenth-century decree by French King Louis XIV: Code Noir. A philosopher in the 1980s described it as "the most monstrous legal text of modern times." It meticulously outlined how enslaved people in French colonies should be treated, from the amount of food they should receive to who would legally own the children born to enslaved women (see p. 12). The document is revolting and as dark as the name it bears, mirroring the entire history of the Caribbean. However, meeting people from the region, you would think differently. They are positive, warm, and cordial, and their food is a delightful product of that dark past. Hence, I couldn't think of a better name for my project than Code Noir. It's time to reclaim the term and flip its connotations. Code Noir no longer stands for oppression; it is a declaration of celebration and hope.

Everything I learned in those early years coalesced in 2020 at Mediamatic, an art and technology center in Amsterdam. There, I hosted a dinner that immersed us in the culinary history of the Caribbean. With special dinnerware, utensils, food, live cooking, and performances, history came alive. The history of the Caribbean islands and the influences of different peoples on the (eating) culture is long and colorful, so I divided history into segments, focusing on four crucial periods in the region leading to the economic, cultural, social, and political changes that make the Caribbean culture what it is today. We examined ingredients and cooking techniques brought by different cultures over the centuries.

The dinner began with a course looking at the indigenous cultures of tribes like the Arawaks, Taíno, and Caribs. At the heart of their diet were tubers, especially the "staff of life": cassava. These tribes differed in their social structures and hierarchies, but they all lived off the islands' abundance, having migrated there from the Americas about two thousand years earlier. They hunted game such as iguanas and guinea pigs and caught fish, ducks, turtles, and other aquatic animals. On small family farms, they grew starchy tubers and beans and more commercial crops like tobacco and cacao beans, which they sold or traded. Common cooking techniques included roasting, smoking, and baking—the now-beloved barbecuing likely originated from "barbacoa," the indigenous method of grilling meat over a fire on wooden stakes. Upon their arrival in the region from 1492 onwards, the Spaniards were said to have been profoundly impressed by the native vegetable gardens, farming techniques, pottery methods, and houses made of plant fibers.

All of this knowledge was brought to life during our *Code Noir* dinner. The meal commenced with an appetizer of cassava roasted over an open fire, to stay as close as possible to the original cooking method. It was accompanied by sweet potatoes cooked in embers, corn relish, lima beans with coconut, and sweet potato chips.

In the second course, we focused on the European influence in the region. The arrival of the Spanish and Portuguese, and later the British, Dutch, and others, brought lemons, limes, coffee beans, grains, vinegar, and livestock—now inseparable elements of Caribbean and South American cuisines. Conversely, the

Europeans were initially suspicious of the food they "discovered" in the region, fearful of transforming into "natives" by eating food they didn't recognize. Corn, for example, terrified them, but they soon relented—ironically, corn has now become one of the world's most important crops. During this part of the dinner, I served coconut "tun"—or as the Italians say, polenta—with roasted pumpkin, caramelized onions, and popped grains.

The next course of the dinner highlighted Africa's impact: many culinary and religious cultural influences in the Caribbean were brought over by enslaved Africans during their dreadful crossing of the Atlantic Ocean. Their customs largely replaced the indigenous knowledge and culture in the area, as the original inhabitants had virtually disappeared by that time, either murdered by Europeans or succumbing to diseases they brought. African cooks were the ones working in the kitchens of the European plantation owners, preparing grand feasts. (Meanwhile, all enslaved workers had to provide their own food. They cultivated crops on makeshift gardens which often barely produced enough to fend off hunger, let alone provide the nutrition needed to endure the hard labor on the land.) Thus, African culinary practices permeated all Caribbean cuisines. From cooking techniques like roasting in leaves, frying, and baking, to spicy, warming stews often featuring New World ingredients. On the *Code Noir* night, we turned the tables. The steamed plantains with spicy tomato sauce, avocados, and peanuts we served are American ingredients that, in turn, crossed the ocean and now symbolize African cuisines.

We concluded the evening with the Asian period, when millions of Chinese and Indians migrated to the Caribbean to work as contracted laborers on the plantations following the abolition of slavery. The contracts provided accommodation, food, and "safety," but most people had no idea what they were getting into. Conditions were harsh, and the work even more so. Familiar food brought comfort. Like the Africans in earlier centuries, the workers brought ingredients from home, like rice—a later staple in the iconic "rice and peas"—and also soy sauce, still found in jerk marinade today. Dahl puri roti, bara, and similar dishes became part of the Caribbean food landscape. The final course of the *Code Noir* dinner consisted of Trini doubles, beloved street food in Trinidad: bara with chickpea curry and a wide array of condiments, such as chutney, chili, and tamarind sauce.

This book is an expansive continuation of the *Code Noir* dinner. I aim to guide you through the vast diversity of cuisine from the Caribbean islands, often birthed under the most challenging conditions imaginable, with unfamiliar ingredients in an inhospitable place. It shows how culinary cultures can evolve, adapt, and ultimately surpass their original forms. *Code Noir* is a tribute to the inventive, displaced cooks, creators, and palate pleasers who each faced their own hardships and yet still managed to create remarkable, joyful, and delicious food.

This is no ordinary ingredient index. Alongside the usual information—how to use, what alternatives are available, and so on—I also offer you historical context, the origins of the dish or ingredient, how it's used in different cultures, and how it made its way to the Caribbean. Through my work with Code Noir, I often challenge people to discover the origins of their food, not only because I find the results fascinating, but also because I believe we can narrate a story from our plate. A tale of journeys, of oppression, victory, triumph, and liberation. And when you look to the past, you can always learn something about the present.

THE
PANTRY

ACHIOTE PASTE AND ANNATTO SEEDS

ACKEE

ACHIOTE

Achiote, or annatto seed, comes from the achiote tree native to the Americas. It has been used for centuries as a food colorant, especially for coloring cheese. The indigenous people of America likely used achiote more for cosmetics than in the kitchen, adorning their faces with it and using it as sunscreen. The Portuguese and Spaniards probably brought the seeds back to Europe. Achiote is sometimes called the poor man's saffron, as it imparts a similar red color. I occasionally use achiote paste not just for its vibrant color, but also for its unique flavor—nutty, peppery, and smoky, with a hint of sweetness. You can purchase achiote paste in tropical supermarkets or online.

ACKEE

The fruit ackee likely traveled from Africa to the Caribbean because enslaved women hid seeds in their hair. Now, ackee is part of Jamaica's national dish: saltfish and ackee (see p. 136). However, if you don't pick and eat ackee at the right time, the fruit can be poisonous. This creamy delicacy—and it is a delicacy, given its price—looks a bit like scrambled eggs but tastes like the creamiest avocado you'll ever savor. Combined with salty bacalhau (cod), sweet bell peppers, and spicy Scotch bonnet, it's truly a dream blend. You can purchase canned ackee from Asian markets that also carry Jamaican products, or online.

ALLSPICE

Allspice, or pimento, originates from the Greater Antilles and South and Central America. In Grenada, the plant's leaves are used like bay leaves, while in Jamaica, allspice branches are laid in the fire for the famous jerk chicken (see p. 142). Allspice is indispensable in this book, being included in nearly all recipes. Also known as Jamaican pepper, it has a faint peppery taste and is often used instead of black pepper in Jamaica. As its English name suggests, allspice carries the aroma of several spices: nutmeg, cloves, cinnamon, and pepper. The berries are slightly larger than juniper berries and can be purchased whole or ground. I prefer to buy whole spices and grind them as needed. The flavor remains robust and aromatic longer this way. Allspice can be found in tropical supermarkets.

BANANA LEAVES

In Caribbean, African, Indian, and Southeast Asian cuisines, the robust leaves of the banana plant are often utilized. While not consumed directly, they're used to envelop ingredients before steaming. When the leaves are scorched over an open flame, they impart a subtle flavor to the packaged ingredients. This cooking technique was likely introduced to the Caribbean islands by enslaved Africans. A similar method of wrapping food in corn husks spread from the Americas to Africa. Banana leaves can be purchased frozen from Asian or African shops.

BLACK-EYED PEAS

Enslaved Africans brought these beans to the Caribbean, and they've become indispensable in a myriad of famous dishes like the fried akkra balls (see p. 80). Originating from West Africa, these are now also beloved in the Caribbean islands and in Brazil. In the state of Bahia, in Brazil, women of African descent sell the fried acarajé balls on the street. You can also use black-eyed peas in recipes that call for kidney beans. Buy them dried (which requires soaking and cooking well in advance) or canned at the supermarket or grocery stores that carry ingredients from tropical locales.

BROWNING

Browning is a sauce added to gravies, stews, curries, and even pies for a deep sweet, nutty taste. It is essentially caramelized sugar taken to the brink of burning. You can buy it ready-made from grocery stores that carry ingredients from tropical locales, online, or make it yourself (see p. 50).

CALLALOO | CARIBBEAN GREENS

CALLALOO | CARIBBEAN GREENS

There's much confusion surrounding callaloo. Is it a specific dish? Or a general term for leafy greens? As far as I've been able to determine, it's a dish made from any green leafy vegetables—whatever is available—with onion, garlic, thyme, and Scotch bonnet. However, the precise recipe varies from island to island and kitchen to kitchen. Nowadays, callaloo is also used as a name for various types of leafy greens used in dishes like oil down and pepperpot soup. Traditionally, amaranth or taro leaves, also known as young dasheen, are used in callaloo. Occasionally, you may find sweet potato leaves used, which can be found in grocery stores that carry ingredients from tropical locales. Alternatively, spinach suffices.

CASSAREEP

This thick, black liquid is made from the juice of grated bitter cassava, which is boiled down to caramel and flavored with spices. It's likely that the original inhabitants of the Caribbean invented it. Cassareep has a preservative effect: when added to pepperpot (see p. 154), you can reuse the leftovers in the pot as long as the cook's lifespan... Find my recipe for cassareep with regular cassava on page 51 or buy it ready-made online or in grocery stores that carry ingredients from tropical locales (also known under the Surinamese name kasripo).

CASSAVA

Cassava is one of the most consumed carbohydrates in the world, especially in Thailand, Nigeria, Indonesia, and Brazil. It contains more starch than potatoes and requires a slightly longer cooking time. Like other starchy tubers, cassava is versatile: it can be boiled, steamed, mashed, roasted, or fried. Cassava is also ground and dried or processed into tapioca, and its liquid is used to make cassareep (as mentioned earlier). Cassava goes by many names, including gari, manioc, arrowroot, and yuca. Most Asian stores—and some supermarkets—sell cassava. They have a brown, thick skin that looks cracked. This is easily removed by cutting the skin lengthwise down to the flesh and using the blunt part of a knife to peel it off.

CHADON BENI | LONG CORIANDER

Also known as cilantro or Mexican coriander, this herb is widely used in the Caribbean. Although the elongated, firm, and serrated leaves look quite different from regular cilantro, they taste similar. Long coriander can sometimes be found in most grocery stores.

CHAYOTE | CHO CHO

Cho cho or chayote, can be found primarily in Asian markets. It is a pear-shaped green vegetable from the cucumber, zucchini, and melon family. Originally from Central America, it is highly versatile: used raw in salads, roasted, or simmered in stews or curries. Its flavor is very mild, somewhat akin to cucumber. When used raw in a dish, it provides a delightful juicy crunch.

CINNAMON

The Caribbean cinnamon varieties are a blend of Ceylon cinnamon and cassia. Cinnamon is widely used in Caribbean dishes, both sweet and savory. It's so common, in fact, that if you simply say "spice" or "hard spice," everyone understands you mean cinnamon. People use the whole sticks or in ground form. Cinnamon is available in all supermarkets.

CASSAVA

CINNAMON

COCONUT

The coconut palm offers abundance. Houses are built from the trunks, ingredients can be cooked in the leaves, ropes are made from the fruit fibers, the water inside the fruit is a supremely refreshing drink, and from the flesh, coconut milk and cream, coconut powder, and coconut flakes are made—all abundantly found in the Caribbean kitchen. The history of coconut is fascinating: the palm comes from Southeast Asia and in early modern times, coconuts were a standard cargo on European ships departing from Asia. The nuts were long-lasting and provided both food (the flesh) and drink (coconut water). Many ships traveling to the West Indies were wrecked in what we now call the Florida Keys. Their cargo, including coconuts, would have drifted to the Caribbean islands, where the locals began to plant the nuts. I prefer to buy coconut milk and cream from the brand Aroy-D or fair trade, which contains plenty of fat.

CONDENSED (COCONUT) MILK

Condensed milk is a source of sweetness and creaminess, and is an indispensable ingredient in candy, desserts, cakes, and drinks. For condensed milk, about sixty percent of the water from milk is evaporated, making it shelf-stable, which was essential for the tropics before the advent of refrigeration. Cans of condensed milk are available at all supermarkets, but some larger ones also have condensed coconut milk—if not, head to Asian markets. Condensed milk is sweet (in fact it's also called sweetened condensed milk) and I use the term interchangeably.

CORN

Thousands of years ago, corn was domesticated in South America. Today, it stands among the top three most cultivated crops in the world. When the Spaniards first tasted corn, they found it unappetizing and only suitable for livestock feed. They feared that eating corn would make them resemble the indigenous peoples. In this book, I use both whole corn kernels (from a can or off the cob) and cornmeal, made from ground dried corn kernels, available in various grinds. Fine cornmeal (often found as polenta in stores) and coarse cornmeal (excellent for breading before frying) can be found in most supermarkets.

CUMIN

Cumin, or jeera as it's called in the Caribbean, became a staple in the West Indian spice cabinet after it was introduced by Indian contract workers. You use the seeds both whole, as in tadka, or ground in curries or aloo pies (see p. 68). The most delicious method is to roast the seeds and grind them yourself.

CURRY | KERRIE

After the abolition of slavery in the British colonies around 1834, the sugarcane plantations faced a labor shortage. Therefore, the British recruited Indians and Chinese as contract workers. They signed contracts for decades and were told they would go to "Chinidad": the land of sugar. Just like the enslaved Africans, these new workers received adapted rations on board the ships crossing the Atlantic Ocean. The ingredients included rice, lentils, ghee, salt, turmeric, onions, and tobacco. They also brought spice mixes: masala, erroneously called "curry" by the Brits. The term curry likely comes from the South Indian Tamil word kari: sauce.

Curry was a seventeenth-century British invention: colonists called all saucy dishes "curry" and wanted to eat them at home in England. They didn't accomplish this by roasting and grinding various spices as their Indian cooks had done, but they invented curry powder: a spice mix in powdered form. In the Caribbean, the spice mix also came to be known as curry. There are various types, but the use of allspice berries in the blend is distinctive. It's used in a multitude of dishes: in chicken curry with roti, or to flavor curry goat (see p. 148). See my version for homemade curry powder on page 50.

GREEN PAPAYA

ALLSPICE

GHEE / VEGAN GHEE

Ghee is a staple in Indian culinary culture and is essentially clarified butter. It is used both for medicinal and culinary purposes. I use ghee in this book for dishes with an Indian influence. There's also vegan vegetable ghee, made from refined palm oil, available in Indian stores or organic supermarkets. Butter-based ghee is also often available at regular supermarkets.

GREEN MANGO

Unripe mango is seen in the Caribbean mainly in dishes influenced by Asian—and specifically Indian—food cultures. I use it to make Trini chow (see p. 218). You can buy the whole fruit in most grocery stores or in Asian or Indian markets.

GUINNESS

The West Indies Porter Guinness is a stout beer from the famed brewery in Dublin. First brewed in 1801, it was specifically crafted for export to the Caribbean, particularly for Irish contract workers—thousands of men, women, and children—who had been sent since the seventeenth century to plantations on the Caribbean islands to cultivate sugar and tobacco. Most were sent to Jamaica, Barbados, Saint Kitts, Nevis, Antigua, and Montserrat, under contracts that ensured their passage, food, clothing, and housing. Sometimes, they were granted a piece of land after their contract's termination date. The West Indies Porter contains more alcohol and hops than the original, to keep the beer in good condition during the four to five weeks of transit across the Atlantic Ocean. The result is a beer rich with flavors of toffee, chocolate, and blackstrap molasses. Savor it neat or use it to make a punch (see p. 237).

HIBISCUS

This flower has many names, including flor de Jamaica, roselle, empire tea, carcade, and sorrel—which in the Caribbean doesn't mean sorrel, but hibiscus. Originating from West Africa, it's said that enslaved Africans, who used it both medically and culinarily, brought it to the other side of the ocean. Hibiscus has a unique flavor: floral and tart with a substantial amount of acidity. A perfect combination with spices and sugar, indeed. You can find dried hibiscus at most Indian markets.

MOLASSES

This dark syrup is a by-product of refining cane or beet sugar and a primary ingredient in most types of rum. Add it to cakes or stews. Like browning (see p. 50), it imparts a sweet taste with a bitter edge.

MUSTARD POWDER

Some of my recipes contain mustard powder as it imparts a delightful sharp kick to dishes. It's available in large supermarkets.

OKRA

Okra, also known as combo, quingombo, malondron, or "lady fingers," plays a crucial role in African, Indian, and Caribbean cuisines. Some people steer clear of it due to its sliminess when improperly prepared. But okra is delightful when cooked well. Originating from Africa and related to corn, it's said that the vegetable reached the Caribbean when Spanish and Portuguese enslaved Africans to cultivate the land. Today, okra is a significant component of Southern food in the United States, especially in gumbo. In the Caribbean, it's used in pepperpot (see p. 154) and cou-cou, sometimes as a thickener in soup or stew. There are two types: dark, long, thin ones used often in Indian dishes and a thick, light green kind seen in the Caribbean. Both types can be used for the recipes in this book, though I suggest choosing the Indian variety for crispy okra (see p. 85). Always look for okra with minimal blemishes. They are sold in grocery stores or African markets.

PALM OIL

Palm oil, while not typically used in Caribbean food, is significant in many West African dishes. And given the West African influences in the Caribbean, I use palm oil quite often in this book. Palm oil was so essential to enslaved Africans that they tried to recreate it on the Caribbean islands with achiote seeds (see p. 32) and coconut oil to mimic its red color. Currently, palm oil often gets bad press, mainly due to the deforestation it causes, putting many animals' natural habitats at risk. However, the main culprit is the bleached, deodorized, and refined palm oil used in industrial products like margarine, cookies, and peanut butter. For West African recipes, you use unbleached and unrefined palm oil, a smaller industry. Purchase good quality, fairly sourced unrefined palm oil, usually found in organic grocery stores.

PAPAYA

Originally from Central America, where it was also domesticated, papaya is used both ripe and green in the Caribbean. It's delicious in juices and hot sauces. The seeds are also edible, with a slightly peppery taste. Supermarkets sometimes sell papayas in winter, while Asian markets usually carry them all year round.

PAPRIKA

Although conventionally recognized as a fruit, these sweet peppers are botanically berries. They are enjoyed in various stages of ripeness: green signifies unripened, then yellow, orange, and red. In the 1920s, Hungary developed a mild variant of the spicy chili pepper, originally from Central America, which became known as paprika. This pepper has since become a staple in Caribbean cuisines, offering a colorful addition to most dishes. Available in any supermarket.

PASSION FRUIT

In the Caribbean islands, passion fruit is predominantly used in juice or syrup over shaved ice, or simply enjoyed pure. Two hundred varieties exist, but four types are most common. The most typical variety sports a purple exterior. The pulp inside is sweet and tart, the seeds slightly peppery. On the French islands, passion fruit is referred to as "maracuja," a name derived from the Tupi word for the fruit. The heavier the fruit, the more juice inside. Select those without blemishes or unsightly spots. Either a smooth or wrinkled skin is fine; the more wrinkled, the sweeter the fruit.

PEANUTS

Originally from South America, peanuts are used less in Caribbean than in African cuisines. Technically not a nut but a legume, the peanut itself is the seed, growing beneath the soil, hence the term "ground nut." If you encounter peanuts in the Caribbean islands, they are more likely to be found in candies and sweet drinks like peanut punch, rather than in savory dishes. I would recommend using unroasted, shelled peanuts for the recipes in this book. For desserts and punch, you can roast and grind the peanuts yourself or purchase peanut butter.

PINEAPPLE

Pineapple is widely used in the Caribbean in pies, candies, drinks, and even hot sauces. You can check if a pineapple is ripe by pulling on its leaves; if they detach easily, the fruit is ready to eat. Refer to page 228 for a more complete history of pineapple.

PLANTAIN

Plantains, plátanos, tostones, patacones, banana da terra—all are names from South and Central America and the Caribbean islands for the same essential ingredient: plantain. You eat them both ripe and unripe, but never raw like their smaller cousin, the banana. Green plantains contain more starch and fiber than ripe, yellow ones. If you fry them at their ripest—when they're almost completely black—they become as sweet as candy. You can also steam or boil them, double-fry and flatten them (tostones), mash them into a purée to accompany fried meat (mofongo), or purée and steam them in a banana leaf (conkies). Bananas originally come from Southeast Asia, and during the Middle Ages, some scholars thought the banana was the forbidden fruit in the Garden of Eden that Eve could not resist. Little is known about the history of plantains, but it's believed that a Spanish bishop brought the fruit from the Canary Islands—where the Portuguese had earlier taken it—to Santo Domingo in 1516. Buy green and yellow plantains at many grocery stores or African markets. They continue to ripen, which is convenient if you can't find them ripe enough.

RED KIDNEY BEANS

The most utilized legume in the Caribbean classic "rice and peas"—and don't ask me why it's not called "rice and beans." Red kidney beans also appear in "stewed peas"—again, not peas. Like most other beans, these originated in the Americas and can be fiery red or speckled white and black. Always cook them, as raw beans are toxic. Soak them overnight in cold water and then cook them in fresh water. They are ready when their skin is no longer wrinkled and they appear plump. Alternatively, you can buy them canned.

RED SNAPPER

This shimmering red fish, as visually appealing as it is palatable, often finds a place at the Caribbean dining table. Despite its meaty texture and numerous bones, don't be deterred: you can often purchase it filleted, or have it cleaned at the fish market. Red snapper sporadically appears in markets; otherwise, you can find it frozen in Asian markets.

RUM

The preferred beverage in the Caribbean and parts of South America, nearly every island has its unique version of this spirit, made from sugarcane juice or molasses. In the sixteenth century, rum was known among pirates as "Kill Devil," and it was the cause of much debauchery in the lawless Port Royal (Jamaica), once known as "the wickedest city in the world." Rum became a significant revenue source for sugarcane plantation owners in the Caribbean. The molasses traveled across the sea to North America and Europe, where it was transformed into rum. Barrels of rum were then used as currency to buy enslaved Africans. The enslaved were given rum to keep them calm, but many accounts show that plantation owners also consumed large quantities. Rum can be as smooth and refined as cognac or brandy, or so strong it burns the throat. An overproof rum simply means the drink contains fifty percent alcohol. White rum is clear and light in flavor, while aged brown rum has a slightly smoky taste and smells of vanilla and molasses.

SALTFISH | BACALAO

Salting and drying fish preserves it for longer. Saltfish in the Caribbean can be made from various types of fish; for bacalao—the word derives from the Portuguese bacalhau—cod is typically used. Saltfish acts as a flavor enhancer in stews, soups, and the iconic bacalao fritters and saltfish with ackee. Purchase bacalao at Asian markets—some supermarkets also carry it—found either on shelves or in the freezer section. Ensure you purchase fish that's already deboned (sometimes sold as fillets), otherwise, you'll spend quite some time removing all the tiny bones. Before use, the fish needs to be partially desalted, which can be achieved by boiling it once or twice or soaking it overnight. See page 130 for a more complete history of saltfish.

SCOTCH BONNET

THYME

SWEET POTATO

SCALLION

An incredibly versatile ingredient in Caribbean kitchens, they emit a milder flavor than onions and play an important role in marinades, green seasoning (see p. 51), and are often stewed whole in rice and peas and soups.

SCOTCH BONNET

Alongside thyme and scallion, I think Scotch bonnet is the most used ingredient in this book. This wrinkly, round chili pepper scores between 100,000 and 350,000 on the Scoville scale—a scale developed by Wilbur Scoville in 1912 to measure the heat of chili peppers (bell peppers are 0, Tabasco sauce 600-800, and the hottest pepper, the Carolina Reaper, is 1,400,000-2,200,000). Although hot, the Scotch bonnet also has a slightly sweet aftertaste that entices you to take another bite. Use the pepper finely chopped or add it whole to give flavor without the heat. I usually buy a bagful because I use them so often. If you have too many, you can freeze them and grate them frozen to add a little kick to your food. They are available in some tropical supermarkets. If you can't find them, use adjuma instead. You may want to wear gloves while handling them and be careful not to touch your eyes.

SCOTCH BONNET, PIMENTO CHILI, MADAME JEANETTE

In the Caribbean, Scotch bonnet and pimento chili are primarily used to add spice to dishes. They bear a resemblance to each other, although pimento chilis are more wrinkled and somewhat longer. They are slightly milder than Scotch bonnets, but the difference is negligible. Usually, they are found in yellow and green. You can purchase Madame Jeanette chili pepper, which closely resembles pimento chilis but is slightly spicier, at tropical supermarkets. They can be easily frozen and grated. You may want to wear gloves while handling them and be careful not to touch your eyes.

SUGAR

In this book, I use various types of sugar, primarily distinguished by their refinement or processing methods. I prefer the least refined versions: brown or raw cane sugar or jaggery, which have more of a caramel flavor. Buy it from organic stores, tropical supermarkets, or online. Refer to page 12 for a more complete history of sugar and its impact on the Caribbean.

SWEET POTATO

Sweet potatoes bring an earthy and sweet flavor to dishes. With more than seven thousand varieties offering a multitude of shapes and flavors, Caribbean kitchens mainly use the Covington variety with its brown skin and orange interior; the batata, brown on the outside and white on the inside; and the Murasaki and Kotobuki, with purple skins and white interiors. The Covington is the most common, but (tropical) supermarkets often carry other types. In my recipes, I'll indicate if a specific variety is needed, but feel free to use Covington if that's all you can find. Sweet potatoes can be boiled, steamed, mashed, roasted, or fried.

TAMARIND

Many backyards in the Caribbean boast tamarind trees, bearing its tart fruit. The pulp, contained in a brown pod interspersed with large seeds, is often ground and incorporated into candies and desserts, sauces, curries, stews, beverages, and chutneys. Its distinctively sour, astringent, and fruity flavor has made it a delicacy in the Caribbean. Originally from Madagascar, tamarind was introduced to Europeans by Arab traders who discovered it in India—referring to it as the Indian date tree. It was subsequently brought to the Caribbean by the Spanish. Tamarind can be found in most supermarkets as a paste, and in Asian shops as a pulp. I use the paste for my tamarind sauce (see p. 213).

THYME

Thyme is one of the most commonly used herbs on the Caribbean islands. Always use fresh thyme, which is readily available in most supermarkets. Even better: purchase a small pot for your balcony or garden.

(BIG) THYME | FIVE-IN-ONE HERB

Also known as "Spanish thyme," we call this herb "big thyme" in Grenada, although it tastes more like oregano—it is also called "Cuban oregano." The Dutch name likely stems from the fact that its taste and aroma are similar to oregano, marjoram, thyme, borage, and mint. The herb has traveled much throughout history: originally from East and South Africa, it spread to India and Southeast Asia. From there, the Spaniards brought it to the Americas. Purchase a plant (organic) for your balcony or garden. If unavailable, substitute with fresh oregano.

YAM

A large tuber with a coarse, brown skin, yams are often used in African cuisines and were likely introduced to the Caribbean by enslaved Africans. Don't be intimidated by its rugged appearance: this tuber could easily compete with the potato. With its earthy and fairly neutral taste, it's perfect for saucy stews. Yams cannot be eaten raw. To test for freshness, squeeze the tuber; it should feel firm.

Here you will find marinades, sauces, and flavorings that form the basis of many Caribbean dishes. Having a few of these jars in your fridge or pantry makes cooking easier and better. In this era of convenience and speed, we often resort to ready-made marinades and spice packets, but these are typically high in salt. Likewise, in many Caribbean home kitchens, you will often find fish and chicken spices in the pantry. Convenient, yes, but never as good as homemade. The time invested is more than worth it, for these foundational recipes yield deeper flavors, rendering your food more complex and delicious. Moreover, the effort is a one-time affair, as a jar lasts for a long time. Essential is the iconic jerk marinade that transforms any meat, fish, or vegetable into a flavor bomb, but also the lesser-known green seasoning that adds depth, taste, and freshness, or which you can serve as a standalone salsa verde. The cassareep and browning, like Worcestershire sauce, are universal flavor enhancers that you'll start adding to all your stews from now on.

BASIC RECIPES

BROWNING

Browning is an essential element in the Caribbean pantry. Like cassareep, it adds depth and a smoky flavor to a dish, courtesy of the burnt sugar used in its preparation. It's indispensable in Jamaican chicken stew and oxtail (see p. 164), but also quite versatile, lending itself well to other stews, soups, and curries.

MAKES APPROXIMATELY ¾ CUP (177 ML)
~ 7 ounces (200 grams) of brown cane sugar
a pinch of salt

YOU'LL ALSO NEED
a sterilized jar with a capacity of approximately ¾ cup (177 ml) (see p. 200)

INSTRUCTIONS

1. Heat the sugar in a saucepan over low to medium heat. Avoid stirring, as this can lead to crystallized sugar lumps. After 10 to 15 minutes, the sugar will start to melt. Begin stirring then, ensuring there are no remaining pieces of undissolved sugar.

2. The sugar will bubble and brown to a mahogany color. As this happens, gradually add about ¾ cup (200 ml) of water. Each time you add water to the pan, step aside to avoid any potential hot caramel splashing. Trust me, you don't want it anywhere near bare skin. Once all the water is added and stirred in, let the caramel thicken for 20 minutes over medium heat.

3. Add a pinch of salt once the browning has the consistency of syrup.

4. Pour into a sterilized jar and store for up to 3 months in the refrigerator.

CARIBBEAN CURRY POWDER

"Curry," is my mother's answer when guests are coming to eat. Even when I was a child and we went to the beach for my birthday, she brought roti and a large, heavy pan of curry, which we had to carry over the dunes; I was mortified. She has embraced the West Indian love for curry. We didn't make our own curry powder at home but bought garam masala or another blend, and my mother swore by Mr. Brown's: a Jamaican blend. Caribbean curry powders differ from Indian ones by the use of allspice and nutmeg, thus forming a perfect marriage between the two cuisines. This is my version.

MAKES APPROXIMATELY 3 ½ OUNCES (100 GRAMS)
1 tablespoon of coriander seeds
1 tablespoon of yellow mustard seeds
½ tablespoon of fenugreek seeds
1 tablespoon of allspice berries
1 tablespoon of cumin seeds
½ teaspoon of cloves
3 teaspoons of ground turmeric
1 teaspoon of ground ginger
1 tablespoon of celery salt (optional)
¼ teaspoon of freshly grated nutmeg
¼ teaspoon of ground cinnamon
¼ teaspoon of coarsely ground black pepper

YOU'LL ALSO NEED
a coffee or spice grinder or a mortar and pestle
a small container or jar

INSTRUCTIONS

1. Toast all whole spices in a dry frying pan over medium heat. Once the spices have filled the air with their fragrance, add the ground spices and mix well.

2. Grind everything finely in a coffee or spice grinder or mortar and pestle.

3. Store in an airtight container or jar. Discard if it no longer gives off any aroma, typically after about 3 months.

CASSAREEP

No pepperpot stew (see p. 154) can come to life without cassareep: a reduction of juice from grated cassava, blended with sugar and spices. This ingenious creation of the original inhabitants of the Caribbean stands as one of the oldest Caribbean condiments.

MAKES APPROXIMATELY 2 OUNCES (60 ML)

6 cassavas (approximately 6 pounds or 3 kilograms)
or 2 pounds (1 kilogram) of frozen grated cassava
2 cloves of garlic
~ 3 ½ tablespoons (20 grams) of grated ginger
1 whole Scotch bonnet pepper
15 cloves
1 teaspoon of coarsely ground black pepper
~ 2 teaspoons (10 grams) of brown cane sugar
1 cinnamon stick
½ teaspoon of salt

YOU'LL ALSO NEED

cheesecloth or tea towel
a sterilized jar with a capacity of approximately
3.5 ounces (100 ml) (refer to p. 200 for details)

INSTRUCTIONS

1. Peel the cassavas (refer to p. 34) and grate them—utilize a grating attachment on your food processor if available. (Or defrost the cassava if you are using frozen grated cassava.) Place the grated cassava in a cheesecloth or tea towel and put it in a bowl. Squeeze out as much juice as you can from the cassava into the bowl. You should yield about 1 and ⅔ cups (400 milliliters) of juice. Allow this juice to sit for 5 minutes so the starch settles at the bottom.

2. Next, carefully decant the juice into a small saucepan, leaving the starch behind in the bowl. Warm the juice over low heat and add the remaining ingredients along with ½ cup (about 100 ml) of water. Increase the heat, stirring continuously until the color shifts from caramel to dark brown. Follow up by adding another ½ cup (about 100 ml) of water. Remove the Scotch bonnet and the cinnamon stick from the pan, then switch off the heat. The sauce should be the consistency of syrup. If it appears too thick, add a bit more water and simmer for an additional 6 to 10 minutes.

3. Finally, strain the sauce into a bowl and transfer to a sterilized jar. The cassareep can be stored for up to 6 months in the refrigerator.

GREEN SEASONING

Upon entering my father's kitchen, I encounter various jars filled with condiments, sauces, and pickles. This is a recipe for a jar brimming with finely chopped green herbs, aptly named green seasoning. It's fairly straightforward and enhances the flavor of everything it touches: use it to marinate chicken before roasting, stir it into stews, soups, or salad dressings, or serve as a dip with snacks. It's hard to find a dish that green seasoning wouldn't complement.

My Aunt Margret-Ann, a noted culinary expert among the double-named inhabitants of the Caribbean islands, is likely one of the finest cooks in my father's family, amid stiff competition from eleven siblings. She always ensures there's a jar of her famed green seasoning in my father's kitchen.

MAKES APPROXIMATELY 3 ½ OUNCES (~ 100 ML)

1 green Scotch bonnet or Madame Jeanette chili pepper
4 sprigs of five-in-one herb or 10 sprigs of fresh oregano
10 sprigs of thyme leaves
7 sprigs of cilantro
8 stalks of parsley (leaves only)
green parts of 4 scallions
~ 2 teaspoons (10 grams) of granulated sugar
2 teaspoons apple cider vinegar
1 ½ teaspoons salt

YOU'LL ALSO NEED

a sterilized jar with a capacity of approximately
½ cup (100 ml)

INSTRUCTIONS

1. Combine all the ingredients with about 1/4 cup (50 ml) of water in a blender and process until smooth.

2. Transfer the mixture to a sterilized jar and store for up to 1 week in the refrigerator.

PEELING CASSAVA

GREEN SEASONING

ROOT VEGETABLES

Root vegetables play a crucial role in Caribbean cuisine. Almost every new culture introduced a new root vegetable to the islands. This includes the native Taíno, Arawak, and Carib peoples who migrated from South, Central, and some believe, even North America. They brought with them cassava and sweet potatoes, which became staple foods for the indigenous population.

When Columbus and his crew arrived on Hispaniola (now Haiti and the Dominican Republic), they were showered with gifts, especially food. They were introduced to "cassava bread." "Bread" was the term the Spaniards used, as it most closely resembled a flat cake made of cassava flour. This "cassava bread" later became a standard ration for sailors crossing the Atlantic Ocean, hence it's also known as the "bread of conquest." This gift inadvertently contributed to the downfall of the gift-givers.

Yams were brought to the Caribbean by West Africans. Traders often brought food onboard ships that the enslaved people were accustomed to, to prevent unrest. The names yam and sweet potato are often confused, likely due to Columbus, who wrote about the sweet potato in his logs. He compared them to carrots, said their taste was similar to chestnuts, and named the root "niames", or yam—a term he knew from Africans in Southern Europe. The Spanish based their word for potato on the Taíno word "batata," which referred to the sweet potato—two different species.

Potatoes are a story of their own. They originally come from Peru, where they were cultivated and domesticated about ten thousand years ago. The Spanish brought them to Europe and over time, the potato became one of the largest and most important crops in the world. Some historians attribute the success of European colonial dominance to the introduction of the humble potato, which led to significant population growth. Portuguese and Dutch traders brought the potato to India in the sixteenth century, but it was during British colonial rule that cultivation and consumption increased: the British believed the potato was a "superior" crop and had it planted all over the subcontinent. This might have seemed like a good deed, but self-interest was the underlying motive: the potatoes were mainly intended for the European market. Potatoes were introduced to the Caribbean by Indian indentured workers, and they can still be found primarily in Indian-inspired dishes.

Root vegetables from all continents often go together in the pan on the Caribbean islands. For example, in the Jamaican "hard food": fish with boiled sweet potatoes, yam, taro, and plantains.

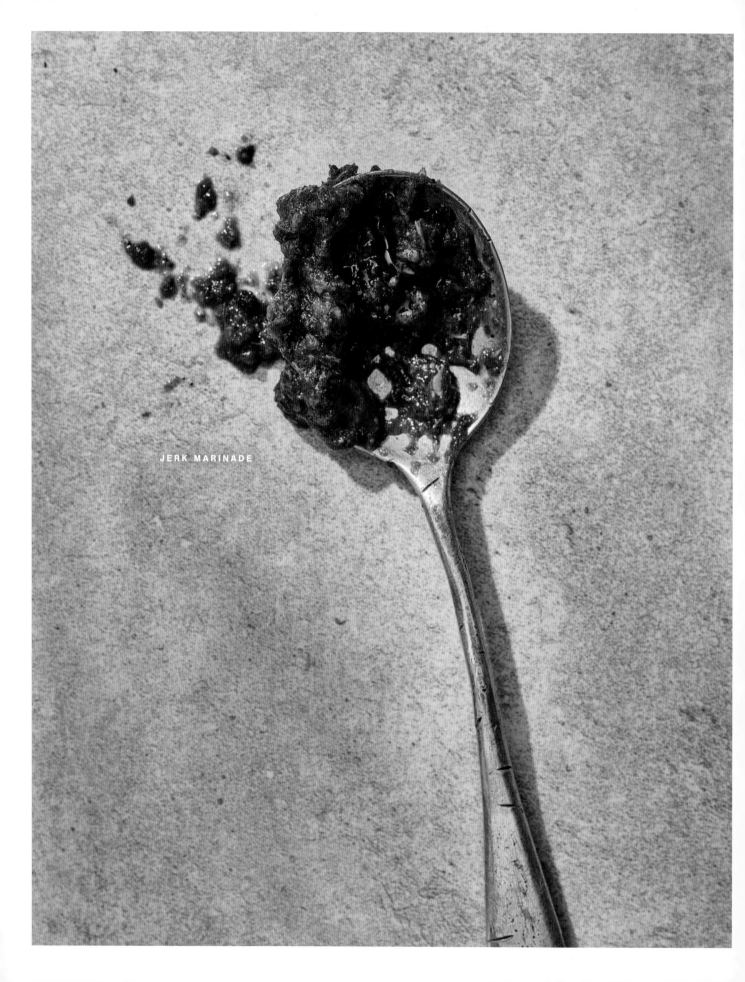

JERK MARINADE

JERK MARINADE

Jerk marinade is a heady blend that fuses the flavors and cooking techniques of indigenous inhabitants and Maroons—enslaved Africans who escaped and established their own communities, complete with their own governance and military, often in collaboration with the original inhabitants. These Maroon communities existed throughout the Caribbean, as well as in Suriname and Brazil. Soy sauce, a distinct influence from the Chinese contract laborers who arrived later, is also used in jerk marinade. Given its complex interplay of spices, herbs, and other flavor enhancers, jerk rightfully boasts an international reputation. While this marinade is traditionally used for the famous jerk chicken (see p. 142), don't hesitate to step off the beaten path: meat and fish also get a wonderful lift from jerk.

MAKES APPROXIMATELY 1 ¼ CUPS (300 ML)

4 shallots

4 cloves of garlic

3 scallions

3 ⅓ tablespoons of ginger

1 Scotch bonnet pepper

20 allspice berries

½ teaspoon of ground cinnamon

1 teaspoon of freshly grated nutmeg

1 teaspoon of smoked paprika

3 teaspoons of dark soy sauce

½ teaspoon coarsely ground black pepper

10 sprigs thyme

1 tablespoon molasses

juice of 1 lime

1 tablespoon of brown cane sugar

YOU'LL ALSO NEED

a sterilized jar with a capacity of approximately 1 ¼ cups (300 ml) (see p. 200)

INSTRUCTIONS

1. Cut the shallots and garlic cloves in half.

2. Heat a dry frying pan over high heat and char the shallots and garlic on all sides, for about 20 minutes. Turn off the heat and let them cool to room temperature.

3. Blend the cooled shallots, scallions, and garlic with the remaining ingredients until smooth.

4. Pour the marinade into a sterilized jar. It can be kept for up to 1 month in the refrigerator.

MOJO

Citrus fruits were introduced to Cuba by Spanish settlers who utilized the juice in marinades, similar to the base used in ceviche, from which mojo was born. I believe the best way to describe this Cuban marinade is as "bright" or clear, sunny, and fresh. Instead of the usual bitter orange juice, I use a mix of lime juice and orange juice. Combined with the herbs, it becomes delightfully tangy, zesty, and herby. I use this marinade on fish (see p. 135) and pork shoulder (see p. 163), but the possibilities are endless.

MAKES APPROXIMATELY 1 ¼ CUPS (300 ML)

3 organic oranges

4 organic limes

7 cloves of garlic

1 onion

2 bunches (30 grams or about 6 tablespoons) of cilantro, leaves only

3 bunches (45 grams or about 9 tablespoons) of oregano, leaves only

1 teaspoon of ground cumin

⅔ cup (150 ml) of olive oil

¼ teaspoon of freshly ground black pepper

2 teaspoons of salt

YOU'LL ALSO NEED

a citrus juicer

a sterilized jar with a capacity of approximately 1 ¼ cups (300 ml) (see p. 200)

INSTRUCTIONS

1. Grate the peel of 1 orange and 1 lime, then squeeze the juice of all the oranges and limes into a bowl.

2. Blend the zest and juice with the remaining ingredients until smooth.

3. Pour the mixture into a sterilized jar and keep for up to 3 months in the refrigerator.

PICKAPEPPA SAUCE

Often referred to as Jamaican ketchup, pickapeppa sauce delights with its versatile flavor, which complements just about anything. The Pickapeppa Company has been crafting this sauce since 1921, following a recipe reputedly created by teenager Norman Nash from Mandeville. A medley of herbs, spices, vegetables, and fruits are combined, then aged in oak barrels to enhance its distinctive taste. Although we'll skip the oak barrel aging in this recipe, rest assured that this marinade will enliven any dish. Traditionally, it's served on a cracker with cream cheese, or used as ketchup on a burger or steak.

MAKES APPROXIMATELY 2 ½ CUPS (600 ML)

2 onions

4 cloves of garlic

2 tomatoes

1 carrot

3 scallions

3 tablespoons of grated ginger

10 sprigs of thyme, stripped

1 organic mango (only the skin is used)

grated peel of 1 large organic orange

1 teaspoon of whole cloves

3 tablespoons of molasses

3 Scotch bonnet peppers

~ ½ cup (70 grams) of black raisins

~ ½ cup (150 ml) of apple vinegar

~ ½ cup (50 grams) of dark brown sugar

YOU'LL ALSO NEED

2 sterilized jars of approximately 1 ¼ cups (300 ml) each (see p. 200)

INSTRUCTIONS

1. Roughly chop the onions, garlic, tomatoes, carrot, scallions, ginger, and thyme. Put them in a food processor. Add the mango skin, orange zest, cloves, molasses, Scotch bonnets, raisins, and vinegar. Blend until a smooth paste is achieved and set aside.

2. Heat the sugar in a large pan over low heat without stirring. Once the sugar crystals start to melt, begin stirring until the caramel achieves a mahogany color, which takes about 15 minutes.

3. Add the paste to the pan and simmer gently over low heat for 20 minutes. Turn off the heat and allow the mixture to cool to room temperature. Transfer to sterilized jars and store in the refrigerator for up to 3 months.

RICE AND PEAS

To have dinner at my father's house on Sunday evening and not serve rice and peas would be sacrilege! Regardless of the rest of the menu, rice and peas are a mainstay. And who could complain? When the rice and beans are seasoned just right and stewed in creamy coconut milk, this dish becomes so delicious that it could stand alone. But where's the fun in that?

SERVES 4-6 PEOPLE

1 large onion

2 cloves of garlic

2 teaspoons of Madame Jeanette chili pepper

2 tablespoons of coconut oil

2 tablespoons of cream of coconut

20 allspice berries

½ teaspoon of coarsely ground black pepper

10 sprigs of thyme

2 vegetable stock cubes

14 ounces (400 grams) of canned red kidney beans in chili sauce

1 ½ cups (300 grams) of basmati rice

1 scallion

1 whole Scotch bonnet pepper

YOU'LL ALSO NEED

a mortar and pestle

INSTRUCTIONS

1. Finely chop the onion, garlic, and Madame Jeanette chili pepper. Heat the coconut oil in a large pan. Combine them with the coconut cream in the pan and sauté until the onions become translucent.

2. Grind the allspice berries into a fine powder using a mortar and pestle. Add them to the pan, along with black pepper, thyme, and vegetable bouillon cubes. Incorporate the beans as well and gently sauté for about 5 minutes, until everything is well mixed.

3. Add the rice to the pan, followed by about 2.5 cups (550 ml) of water. Introduce the Scotch bonnet pepper and whole scallion. Cover the pan and simmer for 30 minutes on low heat until the rice is cooked. Stir once in a while with a metal spoon—a wooden one would compress the rice.

4. As soon as everything is cooked, remove the Scotch bonnet and sprigs of thyme. Although actually made with beans, rice and peas make a delightful accompaniment to any curry or stew in this book.

MAKING ROTI

ROTI (BUSS UP SHUT)

This flatbread with multiple layers is akin to Indian paratha, both crispy and silky. The roti is somewhat torn and messy, hence the name: it is said to resemble a torn T-shirt ("bust up shirt"). The layers are achieved by rolling the dough several times with ghee. It's perfect for scooping up curry or stew. In Trinidad, they eat this roti with choka (see p. 104) for breakfast.

MAKES 6 PIECES
~ 3 cups (350 g) of flour
¾ teaspoon of granulated sugar
1 ½ teaspoons of baking powder
1 teaspoon of salt
½ tablespoon of vegetable (or regular) ghee
⅓ cup (70 g) of ghee

INSTRUCTIONS

1. In a bowl, mix the flour, sugar, baking powder, and salt. Add the ghee and rub together with your thumb and index finger to create a crumbly dough. Gradually knead in a generous ¾ cup (200 ml) of water. Knead on a floured surface to form a smooth dough. Divide into 6 pieces and cover with a damp tea towel. Let it rest for 1 hour.

2. Roll a piece of dough on a floured surface into as thin a circle as possible using a rolling pin. Spread a teaspoon of ghee over it. Cut the dough from the center to the edge, then roll it up into a cone. Fold the tips towards each other to form a ball. Repeat this process with all pieces of dough. Let them sit, uncovered, in the refrigerator for 2 hours on a baking sheet lined with parchment paper, leaving some space between each piece of dough.

3. Heat a large frying pan, preferably a flat roti pan, on low heat. Melt a teaspoon of ghee in it. Remove the dough from the refrigerator and roll one dough ball as thin as possible. Place it in the pan. Roll a clean tea towel into a ball and use it to press down any air bubbles on the roti. Cook the roti for 2 to 3 minutes on each side. Place on a plate and cover with a tea towel. Repeat with the remaining dough balls.

THYME OIL

Thyme oil is a wonderful way to add an herbal note to dishes without the fuss of stripping the leaves.

MAKES APPROXIMATELY ½ CUP (100 ML)
1 bunch (0.5 oz/15 g) of thyme
~ ½ cup (100 ml) of olive oil

YOU'LL ALSO NEED
ice cubes
a coffee filter
a rubber band
a sterilized jar or bottle of approximately ½ cup (about 100 ml) capacity (see p. 200)

INSTRUCTIONS

1. Fill a small pan with water and bring it to a boil. Prepare a large bowl filled with water and ice cubes.

2. Blanch the thyme by immersing it in boiling water for 1 to 2 minutes and then immediately transfer the thyme to the iced water to let it cool. Remove the sprigs from the water, shaking off any excess, and place the thyme (including the sprigs) and the olive oil into a blender. Blend until smooth, about 5 minutes.

3. Secure a coffee filter in a container using an elastic band. Slowly pour the oil through the filter to obtain a clear herbal oil.

4. Store the oil in a sterilized jar or bottle. It will remain good for 2 to 6 weeks.

WHITE RICE

Mastering the art of cooking perfect rice is indeed an achievement. Everyone swears by a specific technique, and if it works for you, carry on. Over the years, I have experimented with various methods, often ending with rice scorched at the bottom of the pan. Until I found this method, where—yes, it is controversial—you do not need to wash the rice. My rice turns out perfectly every time, and hopefully, yours will too from now on.

MAKES 2 SERVINGS

1 cup (200 g) basmati rice

INSTRUCTIONS

1. Combine the rice and 1 ¼ cups (about 300 ml) of water in a small, tall pan. Bring to a boil over medium heat without a lid. As soon as it starts boiling, turn the heat to low and cover the pan. Allow it to simmer gently for 12 minutes.

2. Remove from the heat and let it sit, covered, for 10 minutes. Fluff the rice with two forks and serve.

Caribbean cuisine and culture are deeply intertwined with a sense of togetherness: enjoying a day-long barbecue with friends on the beach, savoring roti at a street stall, or *limin'* (slang for hanging out) with the entire family around a generously filled buffet table. This is why the islands are teeming with bite-sized treats and snacks made for sharing. These small delicacies are packed full of flavor and often come with a spicy kick.

Many of the snacks in this chapter are perfect for sharing with friends at a gathering or party, preferably served freshly made and still piping hot. Some recipes may even become addictive—consider yourself forewarned!

LIMIN':

SHAREABLE BITES

CASSAVA BREAD WITH LIMA BEANS AND CORN RELISH

MAKES 10 PIECES

1 cup (130 grams) of cassava flour (gari)
1 teaspoon salt
2 medium sweet potatoes
1 medium onion
2 cloves of garlic
½ teaspoon of Scotch bonnet pepper, minced
2 tablespoons of olive oil
salt and freshly ground black pepper
1 can (14 ounces/400 grams) of lima beans
1 ounce (35 grams) of coconut cream
3 sprigs of thyme, leaves removed
peanut oil or other vegetable oil for frying
½ teaspoon ground cinnamon

FOR THE CORN RELISH
1 cup (150 grams) corn
½ ounce (15 grams) cilantro
juice of 1.5 limes
¾ ounce (2 grams) Scotch bonnet pepper, minced
salt and freshly ground black pepper, to taste

YOU'LL ALSO NEED
a mandolin
a frying pan
a kitchen thermometer
a slotted spoon

I once created this as an appetizer for a Code Noir dinner, where each course was inspired by prevalent influences or ingredients from a specific moment in Caribbean history (see also p. 21 et seq.). This amuse-bouche was served in honor of the ingredients available to the Caribbean island inhabitants before the arrival of the Spanish: cassava, sweet potatoes, lima beans, and corn. A delightful nibble to serve for a dinner with friends, for example, accompanied by tepache (see p. 232).

INSTRUCTIONS

1. In a bowl, combine the cassava flour with the salt and add about ¼ cups (70 ml) of water. Stir until you have a moist, crumbly dough. Heat a flat pan (roti pan or shallow frying pan) over medium-low heat. Pour some of the gari mixture into the pan in the shape of a circle. Flatten the mixture with a spoon and shape it into a uniform cake about 6 inches in diameter. Cook for 5 minutes, flip, and cookfor another 5 minutes. Place it on a plate and repeat with the remaining cassava dough. Set aside.

2. Preheat the oven to 355°F (180°C). Wash the medium sweet potato and pat dry with kitchen paper. Place in a baking dish and bake for 40 minutes until soft.

3. Place all the ingredients for the corn relish in a food processor and pulse for a few seconds. The relish should be tangy and salty.

4. To prepare the lima beans: finely chop the onion, garlic, and Scotch bonnet. Warm the olive oil in a frying pan and sauté the onion, garlic, and Scotch bonnet until the onion is translucent. Season with salt and pepper. Rinse the lima beans and add to the pan along with the coconut cream and thyme and simmer gently until the coconut cream bubbles and turns light brown. Turn off the heat and adjust the seasoning with salt.

5. Using a mandolin, slice thin slices from the remaining sweet potato. Heat the oil in a frying pan or deep fryer to approximately 340°F (170°C) (use a kitchen thermometer, or drop a piece of bread or the edge of a wooden spoon into the oil: if it immediately sizzles, the oil is hot enough). Fry a few slices of sweet potato for 3 minutes at a time. Use a slotted spoon to remove them from the oil and allow them to drain on a paper towel.

6. Tear the cassava bread into rough strips of approximately 4 by 2 inches. Place in a baking dish and place in the oven for 5 minutes to make them crisp.

7. Remove the soft sweet potato from the oven and cut it in half lengthwise. Scoop out the inside with a spoon and discard the skin. Push the sweet potato through a sieve to create a smooth puree. Add the cinnamon, then season with salt and pepper.

8. Top each piece of cassava bread with 1 tablespoon of sweet potato puree, 1 teaspoon of lima beans, a touch of corn relish, and finish with a sweet potato chip. Your Caribbean treat is ready to be shared and savored!

ALOO PIES

MAKES 10-12 PIECES

FOR THE DOUGH:

4 cups (370 grams) flour, plus extra for dusting

¾ teaspoon salt

¾ teaspoon caster (super fine) sugar

2 teaspoons instant yeast

a dash of oil

FOR THE FILLING:

4 small potatoes

1 small onion

2 cloves garlic

1 teaspoon Scotch bonnet pepper

½ teaspoon fenugreek seeds

½ teaspoon cumin seeds

1 teaspoon ground cumin

2 tablespoons coconut oil

salt and freshly ground black pepper

FOR FRYING:

about 1 quart (1 liter) of sunflower oil or other vegetable oil (such as peanut, coconut, or canola oil)

TO SERVE:

tamarind sauce (see p. 213)

YOU'LL ALSO NEED:

a potato masher

a frying pan

a kitchen thermometer

Aloo pies were invented by East Indian contract workers in the Caribbean—"aloo" means "potato dish" in Hindi. They are a testament to how important it is for diasporic communities to hold onto their cultural (and therefore culinary!) traditions. These pies also represent the ingenuity of those creating a new home: even when certain ingredients weren't available, they came up with something new that some even say is tastier than the original. Aloo pies are no longer just Indian, they're hybrid Indian-Caribbean snacks. The dough balls are filled with fluffy, spicy potatoes—I never knew potatoes could be so delicious. Thanks to a hint of fenugreek and "jeera" (as cumin is called in the Caribbean) and a good kick of Scotch bonnet, you'll find yourself unable to stop eating. Try them with yogurt mixed with a bit of mint as well.

1. Place the flour, salt, sugar, and yeast in a bowl and mix well. Gradually add approximately 1 ¼ cups (300 ml) of water while kneading. Lightly dust a workspace with flour. Knead the dough on this surface for 10 to 15 minutes until it is as smooth and pliable as bread dough. Lightly grease a bowl with a bit of oil, place the dough in it, and cover with a damp kitchen towel. Allow to rest for 1 hour.

2. Peel the potatoes and cut them into approximately ¾-inch cubes. Place them in a pot of water and bring to a boil. Cook until they fall apart when poked with a knife, about 20 minutes. Drain the potatoes and set aside.

3. Finely chop the onion, garlic, and Scotch bonnet, then set aside.

4. Toast the fenugreek seeds, cumin seeds, and ground cumin in a dry frying pan for about 2 minutes, until they begin to release their aroma. Add the coconut oil, onion, garlic, and Scotch bonnet and sauté until lightly golden brown. Transfer the onion mixture to a blender or food processor and pulse for a few seconds. Add this mixture to the potatoes and mash with a potato masher (or a fork) until you have a coarse puree. Season with salt and pepper.

5. Form a ball of dough about 1 ounce (30 grams) and flatten it with your hands to a disc about 5 inches in diameter. Place a generous teaspoon of the potato filling in the center and fold the dough over it. Seal by firmly pressing the edges between your thumb and index finger, ensuring there's no air trapped inside the pie. You can neatly fold the edge, or make indentations with a fork, but the most important thing is that the dough is sealed well to prevent the filling from escaping during frying. Repeat this process to make all the aloo pies.

6. Place a deep pan on the stove and fill it with the oil. Heat over medium heat to about 340 degrees Fahrenheit (use a kitchen thermometer, or drop a piece of bread or the edge of a wooden spatula into the oil: if it immediately bubbles, the oil is hot enough). Fry the aloo pies in batches for 3 minutes on each side, until golden brown. Remove from the pan and drain on paper towels.

7. Serve with tamarind sauce. Enjoy your cooking journey and the delicious taste of these unique, cultural aloo pies.

There is nothing quite like roasted corn on the cob, and these "ribs"—think of them as similar to spare ribs—are no exception. But the figurative cherry on top is the jalapeño butter with scallions that I could happily eat all day. And then there's the feta and cilantro on top! This is a superb side dish, serve it for example with the jerk chicken on page 142, or place it on the table with a number of other small dishes to share with friends.

INSTRUCTIONS

1. Preheat the oven to 350°F (175°C) .

2. Remove the leaves from the corn cobs and cut off a piece from the bottom to make it flat. Use a sharp knife and cut one cob in half lengthwise. Then halve these halves lengthwise again to get 4 long quarters. Repeat with the other corn cob. Set aside.

3. In a bowl, combine the olive oil, honey, thyme, and spices. Season with salt and pepper. Generously coat each piece of corn with the oil mixture. Place them on a baking sheet and roast in the oven for about 20 minutes, until the corn gets brown edges.

4. Meanwhile, prepare the scallion-jalapeño butter: coarsely chop the scallion and strip the thyme. Combine with the remaining ingredients in a food processor and grind for 1 minute. Spoon into a bowl and season with salt and pepper.

5. Brush the corn ribs with the scallion-jalapeño butter and sprinkle with the crumbled feta, lime zest, juice, and cilantro. Enjoy this flavorful delight.

CORN RIBS WITH SCALLION-JALAPEÑO BUTTER

MAKES 2 SERVINGS

2 cobs (or ears) of corn
5 tablespoons of olive oil
2 tablespoons of honey
4 sprigs of thyme, leaves removed
2 teaspoons smoked paprika
1 teaspoon cayenne pepper
1 teaspoon garlic powder
salt and freshly ground black pepper
~ 1 tablespoon (10 g) of feta cheese, crumbled
grated zest and juice of 1 organic lime
⅓ cup (10 g) of cilantro, coarsely chopped

FOR THE SCALLION-JALAPEÑO BUTTER
1 scallion
5 sprigs of thyme
~ 3 ½ tablespoons (50 g) of butter
1-½ fresh jalapeño pepper
salt and freshly ground black pepper

Growing up, I was enamored with these crunchy delights. All those textures come together unbelievably well: crispy on the outside, soft with a spicy kick on the inside. I was hooked. Alas, my father never wanted to make them. I think he, like many others, didn't want to deal with the fuss of frying. So, I had to patiently wait until we visited my Aunt Margret-Ann. She would invite us for brunch and serve these saltfish fritters, along with other Grenadian classics like saltfish souse and bakes. I would devour as many fritters as my little stomach could handle. Now that I am an adult, I can make them to my heart's content. And when I do, I revert back to my childlike behavior and stuff myself silly.

INSTRUCTIONS

1. Place the saltfish in a pan with cold water and bring it to a boil. Cook for 20 minutes, skimming off the salty foam that surfaces. You want to remove some of the salt, not all. Drain the fish and taste: it should still be slightly salty, but not overly so. If it is unpleasantly salty, boil the fish for another 20 minutes in fresh water.

2. Meanwhile, roughly chop the bell pepper, onion, scallions, and garlic. Put them in a blender along with the parsley (including stems). Strip the thyme leaves and add them. Pulse until well incorporated. Scoop into a bowl and mix in the paprika, black pepper, milk, and ketchup. Finely chop the Scotch bonnet pepper and stir in. Season with salt and pepper and set aside.

3. In a separate large bowl, mix the flour with the baking powder. Add the vegetable mixture and 2 75ml sparkling water, alternatively still water is also fine. After allowing it to cool, flake the saltfish, removing any bones, and add to the bowl. Stir well.

4. Heat the sunflower oil in a deep frying pan to about 340-360°F (170°C) (use a kitchen thermometer, or drop a piece of bread or the edge of a wooden spoon in the oil: if it immediately sizzles, the oil is hot enough). Scoop a tablespoon of batter from the bowl and carefully lower it into the oil. Fry the saltfish fritters in batches for about 3 to 4 minutes on each side. Remove them with a slotted spoon and drain on a paper towel.

5. Enjoy them as is, or serve with a dip, such as the pineapple-chili sauce on page 218.

SALTFISH FRITTERS

MAKES APPROXIMATELY 16 PIECES

5 ounces (about 150 g) of saltfish fillets
½ red bell pepper
½ small onion
2 scallions
1 clove of garlic
1 cup (15 g or ~ ½ ounce) of flat-leaf parsley, approximately 1 small bunch
4 sprigs of thyme
½ teaspoon of smoked paprika
⅛ teaspoon of freshly ground black pepper, plus extra to taste
2 teaspoons of (oat) milk
2 teaspoons of ketchup
1 Scotch bonnet pepper (approximately 5g, or about 1.5 to 2 teaspoons when finely chopped)
salt to taste
1 cup (100 g) of flour
2 ½ teaspoons of baking powder
75ml sparkling water
2 cups (500 ml) of sunflower or other vegetable oil, for frying

YOU'LL ALSO NEED
a slotted spoon
a deep frying pan
a kitchen thermometer

PEPPERED SHRIMP

MAKES 3-4 SERVINGS

2 large garlic cloves
2 Scotch bonnet peppers
10 ounces (about 300 g) of medium fresh
shrimp, unpeeled
½ tablespoon of cayenne pepper
1 tablespoon of smoked paprika
1 tablespoon of achiote paste
salt and freshly ground black pepper
to taste
½ teaspoon of yellow split pea flour
1 ½ tablespoon coconut oil

This Jamaican street food is typically purchased in plastic bags: the shrimp bathe in a bright red-orange powder. The red color comes from achiote paste, also known as annatto seed (see p. 32). They're blazing hot, though not so much to keep you from reaching for another one. And another. But be careful! Don't touch your eyes while cooking or eating the shrimp.

INSTRUCTIONS

1. Finely chop the garlic and Scotch bonnets, then place them in a sandwich or freezer bag along with the shrimp, cayenne pepper, smoked paprika, achiote paste, and salt and pepper to taste. Shake the bag to distribute the marinade evenly. Allow it to marinate in the refrigerator for 24 hours.

2. Mix the yellow split pea flour into the shrimp, ensuring all the shrimp receive a coating.

3. Heat the coconut oil in a frying pan and sauté the shrimp for approximately 5 minutes, stirring occasionally to prevent the spices from burning.

Nearly every culture possesses a tradition of cooking in leaves. These pasteles are the Caribbean's contribution. They truly symbolize Christmas cuisine, a time when the family congregates and painstakingly fills and folds these packets on a sort of assembly line. Yes, it's time-consuming, but the result is more than worth the effort.

Variations exist all across Latin America and the Caribbean—Venezuela, Mexico, Colombia, Trinidad, and even Pacific countries. As with many dishes, the ingredients vary based on local availability. Although the name often changes, the basic premise remains the same: a cornmeal dough filled with spiced meat, wrapped in a banana leaf, and cooked.

The Caribbean pasteles were likely invented by the Taíno, who originally wrapped them in corn husks—banana leaves were introduced later from Asia—and they may have offered them to Columbus. Theories also exist about the influence of enslaved Africans on pasteles, as the technique of cooking food in banana leaves has been commonplace in West Africa for centuries. The Europeans introduced meat and ingredients like capers, olives, and raisins. While there is much speculation about the exact origin of pasteles, one can confidently assert they're worthy representatives of the Caribbean culinary melting pot. Serve them with green seasoning to add a touch of freshness.

PASTELES

MAKES 15 PASTELES

FOR THE FILLING
1 medium onion
3 cloves of garlic
1 tablespoon of grated ginger
~ 2 tablespoons (30 g) of black raisins
~ 3 tablespoons (40 g) of pitted mixed olives
~ 1 teaspoon (10 g) of capers
2 tablespoons of coconut oil
¼ teaspoon of frozen grated Scotch bonnet pepper (see p. 42)
10 ½ ounces (300 g) of mixed ground meat
2 tablespoons tomato paste
3 tablespoons green seasoning (see p. 51)
2 teaspoons achiote paste
5 sprigs of thyme
8 leaves of oregano
2 tablespoons of Worcestershire sauce
salt and freshly ground black pepper

FOR THE DOUGH
13 ounces (365 g) of pre-cooked yellow cornmeal
~ ¼ cup (60 g) of clarified butter, lard, or vegetable ghee
6 tablespoons of coconut oil
1 teaspoon of salt
3 ½ cups (1 litre) of vegetable broth

ADDITIONALLY:
10 banana leaves
a drizzle of olive oil
1 recipe of green seasoning, to serve (see p. 51, optional)

YOU'LL ALSO NEED
a steamer pan

INSTRUCTIONS

1. Finely chop the onion, garlic, and ginger. Dice the raisins, olives, and capers. Heat the coconut oil in a frying pan and sauté the onion, garlic, ginger, and Scotch bonnet until the onion becomes translucent. Add the ground meat and cook for 2 minutes. Add the raisins, olives, and capers and cook for another 2 minutes until the meat begins to brown. Add the tomato paste, achiote paste, thyme, oregano, Worcestershire sauce, and 3 tablespoons of water. Sauté for 10 minutes on low to medium heat. Season with salt and pepper. Remove from heat and set aside.

2. Put the cornmeal in a bowl. Distribute the clarified butter and coconut oil over it, then add the salt. Combine with your fingers to a crumbly dough. Add the vegetable broth and mix well with a spoon. Set aside and cover with a damp tea towel.

3. Rinse the banana leaves, pat them dry, and cut them so they are 3 inches wide. If you have a gas stove, briefly hold each leaf above the flame—this allows the pasteles to absorb the scent and flavor of the banana leaf. Use a pastry brush to lightly coat the insides of the leaves with some olive oil.

4. Roll an approximately ¾ cup (70 g) ball of dough and place it in the middle of a strip of banana leaf. Fold a part of the leaf over the dough. Press the dough flat with a plate, forming a thin, circular piece of dough about 4 inches in diameter.

5. Unfold the leaf and place 2 tablespoons of filling in the center of the dough. Now, you'll close the pasteles, using the banana leaf as a tool: grab the leaf and fold one side of the dough to the middle. Repeat this on the other side and at the top and bottom. You now have a closed dough packet. Then roll the leaf around the dough and fold the top and bottom tightly. Tear a strip from the edge of the banana leaf and use it to tie the packet closed. Prepare all pasteles in this way.

6. Place all the folded pasteles in a steamer. Alternatively, you can place a colander or sieve over a pot of boiling water. Steam for 20 to 30 minutes until the dough is cooked. Unwrap the pasteles and serve with the green seasoning.

AKKRAS (BLACK-EYED PEA FRITTERS)

MAKES 20 PIECES

1 ½ cups (250 g) dried black-eyed peas

1 large shallot

2 garlic cloves

½ teaspoon Scotch bonnet pepper

4 sprigs of thyme, stripped

½ bunch of cilantro

3 tablespoons flour (optional)

salt and freshly ground black pepper

2 cups (500 ml) sunflower oil or other vegetable oil for frying

1 recipe of tomato sauce with dried shrimp (see p. 222)

YOU'LL ALSO NEED

a frying pan

a kitchen thermometer

This snack goes by many names, just like many other dishes that crossed the Atlantic Ocean and are still eaten on both sides. In Nigeria, you ask for acaraje or akara, in Senegal it's accara, koose in Sierra Leone, akla in Ghana, acarajé in Brazil, and acras de zieu noi's in Martinique. The main ingredients and preparation of deep-fried balls of black-eyed peas are the same everywhere. Perhaps the most fascinating aspect of this dish—and many other street foods—is that akkras represented financial independence for many enslaved women.

In some colonies, plantation owners temporarily gave plots of land to the enslaved, where they could grow their own food. If there was a surplus—which wasn't often—the women were permitted to go to the market on Sundays to sell their products. The proceeds often had to be handed over to the plantation owner, but sometimes the women were allowed to keep the profits. After the abolition of slavery, selling snacks like akkras remained an important source of income for women, who thereby earned a living and supported their families.

INSTRUCTIONS

1. Soak the peas overnight in a bowl of water. Drain them and place them under clean, now warm water. Let them stand for another hour.

2. Rub the beans between your fingers to remove the skins, which is easier if you refresh the water several times, causing the skins to float to the top. Once you have removed as many skins as possible, carefully pour off the top layer of water with the skins. Then drain the remaining water. Scoop the skinned beans into a food processor.

3. Finely chop the shallot, garlic, and Scotch bonnet, and add to the food processor. Add the thyme leaves, the stems and leaves of the cilantro, and a teaspoon of warm water. Process until a fine, smooth paste forms. If it's too liquid, add some flour. Season generously with salt and pepper.

4. Heat the oil in a pan to about 340°F (170°C) (use a kitchen thermometer, or drop a piece of bread or the edge of a wooden spoon into the oil: if it sizzles immediately, the oil is hot enough). Using two spoons, shape an oval ball (quenelle) of the bean mixture and gently lower it into the oil. Turn after 2 minutes, ensuring all sides brown nicely. Remove from the pan with a slotted spoon and drain on paper towels. Continue to make and fry all the akkra in batches.

5. Serve them with tomato sauce for dipping.

CRISPY OKRA

Not everyone is a fan of okra, due to the sliminess it can emit into stews and soups. But fear not: when okra is prepared in this manner, it turns supremely crispy.

INSTRUCTIONS

1. Wash the okra and trim off the tops. Pat the okra dry with kitchen towel, cut them in halve, then set aside. Mix all the spices together with the rice flour and season the okra, along with a generous helping of salt. Leave to marinade for 30 minutes. Heat the oil in a pan over medium heat and fry the okra for about 3 minutes, until crispy.

2. Serve with spicy mayo.

CRISPY OKRA

MAKES 2 SERVINGS

~ ½ cup (100 grams or approximately 10-15 pods, depending on size) of okra
2 tablespoon of rice flour
1 teaspoon chili powder
1 teaspoon ground cumin
1 teaspoon smoked paprika powder
¼ teaspoon of salt
¼ cup (50 ml) of sunflower or other vegetable oil
1 spicy mayo recipe, for serving
(see p. 222)

Corn fritters are a true go-to snack in both the Caribbean and the southern United States. With an abundance of corn, these addictive snacks can be whipped up in no time. My recipe incorporates more vegetables than most Caribbean versions; a tasty, healthy balance amid all that frying. Serve them as a snack or alongside a main dish.

INSTRUCTIONS

1. Cut the corn kernels from the cobs and place in a bowl. Finely chop the red pepper, scallions, Scotch bonnet, and celery, and add to the corn.

2. Mix in the spices, thyme leaves, flour, and cane sugar well, then season generously with salt and pepper.

3. Heat the oil in a deep (frying) pan to about 340°F (170°C) (use a kitchen thermometer, or drop a piece of bread or the edge of a wooden spoon into the oil: if it sizzles immediately, the oil is hot enough). Scoop a tablespoon of the batter into the oil and fry for 4 minutes on each side, until the fritter is nicely browned. Remove from the pan with a slotted spoon and drain on paper towels. Continue frying all the fritters in batches until the batter is gone.

4. Enjoy them as they are or serve with the spicy mayonnaise from page 222, for example.

CORN FRITTERS

MAKES 12 FRITTERS

2 ears of corn (pre-cooked)
~ ⅓ cup (50 grams) of red bell pepper
2 scallions
~ ½ Scotch bonnet (2 grams) pepper
1 celery stalk
¾ teaspoon of smoked paprika
⅛ teaspoon of ground cumin
¼ teaspoon of cayenne pepper
3 sprigs of thyme leaves
¾ cup of flour
½ teaspoon brown cane sugar
salt and freshly ground black pepper
⅔ cup (150 ml) of sunflower or other vegetable oil (such as peanut, coconut, or rapeseed) for frying

YOU'LL ALSO NEED
a pan for frying
a kitchen thermometer
a slotted spoon

CASSAVA FRIES

MAKES 3-4 SERVINGS

2 ¼ pounds (1 kilogram) of cassava
3 cups (700 ml) of sunflower or other
vegetable oil, for frying
salt and freshly ground black pepper
to taste

YOU'LL ALSO NEED
a frying pan
a kitchen thermometer
a slotted spoon

Cassava fries make a terrific alternative to traditional potato-based fries. They boast a richer flavor, with a sweet, almost nutty taste. My method of preparation gives them a supremely crispy exterior while keeping them light and fluffy on the inside. Enjoy!

INSTRUCTIONS

1. Peel the cassava (see pp. 34, 52) and cut it crosswise into 4-inch pieces. Place them in a pan and cover with salted water. Bring to a boil and cook for approximately 20 minutes, or until you can easily pierce them with a fork.

2. Drain and let cool.

3. Halve the pieces lengthwise and remove the fibrous core. Slice the pieces into fries about ½ inch thick.

4. Heat the sunflower oil in a frying pan to about 340-360°F (170-180°C) (use a kitchen thermometer, or drop a piece of bread or the edge of a wooden spoon into the oil: if it immediately sizzles, the oil is hot enough). Fry the cassava in small batches to prevent the oil from cooling down. Remove them from the pan with a slotted spoon once the cassava fries turn golden brown and drain on paper towels.

5. Season with salt and pepper and serve with a dipping sauce. I recommend the spicy mayo (see p. 222).

At times, my fruit bowl sadly harbors withering black plantains. I have an absolute aversion to food waste, so I never discard them. Moreover, I adore plantains at the end of their life, because the blacker the fruit, the more the starch has developed, thus rendering it sweeter. This contrasts perfectly with spicy food.

You could slice the bananas and fry them in oil, but one day I decided to mash them and roll them in polenta for a delightful crunch, inspired by a dish I had eaten at my Aunt Rosie's. I served them during a dinner party where they were such a roaring success, particularly with my friend's daughter and son, that barely anything was left for us.

INSTRUCTIONS

1. Peel the plantains. Place them in a bowl and mash with a potato masher (or a fork) into a pulp. Add the flour and season with salt and pepper to taste. Cover the mixture and refrigerate for 30 minutes.

2. Sprinkle the polenta on a plate.

3. Remove the plantain mixture from the refrigerator and roll it into 1-inch balls. If the mixture is too wet, you can add another teaspoon of flour. However, resist the temptation to add much more, as this will result in mealy balls.

4. Roll the balls in the polenta. If they are still very wet, place them back in the refrigerator for another 30 minutes.

5. Heat the sunflower oil in a deep frying pan to about 340-360°F (170-180°C) (use a kitchen thermometer, or drop a piece of bread or the edge of a wooden spoon into the oil: if it sizzles immediately, the oil is hot enough). Now, work quickly: roll the balls in the polenta once more and carefully lower them into the hot oil. Fry the balls in batches for about 3 minutes on each side. Remove them from the pan and drain them on paper towels.

6. Enjoy them as they are or serve them with a chili sauce for dipping, for instance, the one on pages 225 or 218.

PLANTAIN BALLS

MAKES 8 PIECES

2 overripe plantains (the blacker, the better)
2 ½ tablespoons of flour
salt and freshly ground black pepper
½ cup (50 grams) of polenta
1 ¼ cups (250 ml) of sunflower oil

YOU'LL ALSO NEED
a potato masher
a kitchen thermometer

A few summers ago, I came up with this snack while hosting a pop-up. Unfortunately, the weather didn't cooperate, with rain pouring down each of the four weekends I planned to cook there. Despite the rain, I wanted to create something featuring the iconic Caribbean rice and peas, but in a format that would be easy to enjoy standing, perhaps with a glass of Aperol in the other hand. That's how these rice and peas arancini were born, served with papaya chili sauce. They were such a hit that everyone asked me for the recipe, but I'd crafted them intuitively, without jotting anything down—until now. The lemon and parsley lend the arancini a fresh flavor, and the panko adds a crunchy layer. They are truly, incredibly delicious, come rain or shine.

RICE AND PEAS ARANCINI

MAKES 9 PIECES

~ 2 ½ cups (300 grams) of rice and peas (recipe on p. 58)
1 ¼ ounces (50 grams) of Parmesan cheese
½ teaspoon of garlic powder
½ teaspoon of smoked paprika
1 bunch (15 grams) of flat-leaf parsley
Zest of 1 organic lemon
2 tablespoons of coconut cream
1 vegetable bouillon cube
1 egg
salt and freshly ground black pepper
2 cups (500 ml) of sunflower oil or other vegetable oil, for frying
2 ounces (50 grams) of panko breadcrumbs
1 recipe for papaya chili sauce, to serve (see p. 223)

YOU'LL ALSO NEED
a potato masher
a frying pan
a kitchen thermometer

INSTRUCTIONS

1. Combine the rice and peas in a bowl with the Parmesan cheese, garlic powder, smoked paprika, parsley, lemon zest, and coconut cream. Dissolve the vegetable bouillon cube in a bowl with about ½ cup (100 ml) of boiling water and add 10 teaspoons to the rice mixture (you won't need the rest). Beat the egg and add it to the bowl. Using a potato masher, combine the ingredients into a sticky consistency—but not too much, as you want to preserve the texture of the beans. Season with salt and pepper. Then put the rice mixture in the fridge for 1 hour, until it's chilled.

2. Using a tablespoon or small ice cream scoop, portion out the mixture and shape it into balls.

3. Heat the oil in a pan to about 340°F (170°C) (use a kitchen thermometer, or drop a piece of bread or the side of a wooden spoon into the oil. If it immediately sizzles, the oil is hot enough).

4. Meanwhile, spread the panko breadcrumbs on a plate. Roll the rice balls in the panko and carefully drop them into the hot oil. Do not fry too many at once, as this can lower the oil's temperature too quickly. Fry the balls for about 5 minutes, turning them regularly so they brown evenly on all sides. Remove them from the pan with a slotted spoon and let drain on paper towels.

5. Serve with the papaya chili sauce.

Hungry and short on time? Not a great combination, particularly if you get as "hangry" as I do. But fear not. In this chapter, I'll help you with quick recipes. Later in this book, I write about the importance of taking your time in the kitchen, but I promise you: these dishes do not compromise on flavor. So, if you're in a hurry and still crave authentic Caribbean flavors, quickly flip through this chapter. Vegetarian, meat, fish, stews, and curries: you'll find them all here.

EVERY-DAY EATS

VEGETARIAN / MEAT / FISH

VEGETARIAN

COCONUT DAHL

MAKES 6 SERVINGS

FOR THE DAHL

2 medium onions

4 cloves of garlic

a thumb-size piece (20 grams) of ginger, peeled

1 ¼ cups (250 grams) of red lentils

3 tablespoons of coconut oil

4 tablespoons of Caribbean curry powder (see p. 50)

3 fresh curry leaves (optional)

~ 1.5 tablespoons (20 grams) of coconut cream

1 ¾ cups (400 ml) of coconut milk

salt and freshly ground black pepper

1 tablespoon of coconut flakes

FOR THE TADKA

1 clove of garlic

1 shallot

1 tablespoon of ginger, peeled

3 tablespoons of ghee or coconut oil

4 dried rawits (small, hot chili peppers, also known as bird's eye chilies) or dried red peppers

1 teaspoon smoked paprika

1 teaspoon cumin seeds

2 fresh curry leaves

This is a delightful dish for weekdays when you don't want to eat meat. Despite the significant Indian influence there, dahl isn't eaten much in the Caribbean. It's a pity, as it is a quick, easy, and inexpensive meal option. And delicious: this version is full of warm and deep flavors. The tadka with chewy garlic and shallots that you pour over it at the end elevates it even further.

INSTRUCTIONS

1. To prepare the dahl, finely chop the onions, garlic, and ginger and set aside. Rinse the red lentils in a sieve under running water until the water is clear.

2. Heat a large, heavy-bottomed pan over medium heat. Melt the coconut oil in it and sauté the onions, garlic, ginger, curry powder, and curry leaves until the onions are golden brown. Add the coconut cream and mix well. Then add the red lentils, coconut milk, and 1 ⅔ cups (400 ml) of water to the pan. Simmer over low heat for 45 minutes, stirring regularly. Season with salt and pepper.

3. Meanwhile, toast the coconut flakes in a dry frying pan over medium heat for about 2 minutes until the flakes begin to turn lightly golden brown and smell fragrant. Set aside.

4. To prepare the tadka, finely chop the garlic, shallot, and ginger. Heat the ghee or coconut oil in a small pan for 5 minutes—the oil must be very hot before you add the rest of the ingredients. Add the shallot, garlic, ginger, rawit pepper, paprika, cumin seeds, and curry leaves to the pan and sauté until the garlic is brown, about 5 minutes. Be careful not to burn the garlic and shallot, as it would make the tadka bitter.

5. Serve the dahl in a bowl or the pan. Pour the tadka over it and finish with the toasted coconut flakes.

6. Serve with rice or roti (see p. 60).

This dish, literally "stewed peas" (but actually beans), is of paramount importance in Jamaica, and you'll find various versions on other Caribbean islands. I find it remarkable that such a humble and inexpensive ingredient as beans can be transformed into such a tasty, warming, and filling meal. I've left out the usual salted meat, so that vegetarians and vegans can also enjoy the peas. You're supposed to use dried beans that have been soaked overnight, but I use canned beans: it's quicker and makes for an easy midweek dinner. The spinners (dumplings) on top are the metaphorical icing on the cake.

INSTRUCTIONS

1. Finely chop the onions, garlic, ginger, shiitake mushrooms, and Scotch bonnet pepper. Heat the coconut oil in a large, heavy-bottomed pan over low heat. As soon as the oil is hot, add the chopped ingredients and sauté for 3 to 5 minutes, or until the mixture turns golden brown. Add the coconut cream to the pan and mix well. Drain the kidney beans and add to the pan, along with the coconut milk, cinnamon, thyme, pepper, bouillon cube, and 2 tablespoons (30 ml) of water. Let it simmer gently.

2. Meanwhile, prepare the spinners: in a bowl, mix the flour with a pinch of salt and 3 tablespoons of water. Knead into a smooth dough. Take a piece of dough the size of a quarter and roll it in the palm of your hand into an elongated dumpling. Repeat with the rest of the dough to make all the spinners. Place them on top of the beans in the pan and let them cook, uncovered, over low heat for about 45 minutes to 1 hour. Taste and add salt if necessary.

3. Serve with white rice and fried banana.

STEWED PEAS WITH SPINNERS

MAKES 4 SERVINGS

2 onions
3 cloves of garlic
~ 1 tablespoon (5 grams) of ginger, peeled
~ ½ cup (50 grams) of shiitake mushrooms
1 Scotch bonnet pepper
2 tablespoons of coconut oil
~ 5 tablespoons (70 grams) of coconut cream
1 can (14 ounces) of red kidney beans
¾ cup (200 ml) of coconut milk
1 cinnamon stick
6 sprigs of thyme
½ teaspoon of coarsely ground black pepper
1 vegetable bouillon cube
½ cup (60 grams) of flour
a pinch of salt

BAIGAN CHOKA WITH COCONUT TUN (ROASTED EGGPLANT AND COCONUT POLENTA)

MAKES 4 SERVINGS

2 eggplants (approximately 18 ounces or 500 grams)
1 tomato
3 cloves of garlic
¾ teaspoon of vegetable ghee (or clarified butter)
¾ teaspoon of ground cumin
¼ teaspoon of smoked paprika powder
⅛ teaspoon of frozen grated Scotch bonnet pepper (see p. 42)
salt and freshly ground black pepper

FOR THE COCONUT TUN
¾ cup (200 ml) of coconut milk
~ ¾ cup (150 grams) of fine polenta
1 vegetable bouillon cube
3 tablespoons of cream cheese
~ ½ cup (100 grams) of Parmesan cheese, grated
¼ teaspoon mustard powder
¼ teaspoon freshly grated nutmeg
salt and freshly ground black pepper

FOR THE TADKA
1 shallot
1 clove of garlic
¼ ounce (5 grams) of ginger
½ cup (120 ml) of vegetable ghee (or clarified butter)
~ ½ teaspoon (2 grams) of dried rawit or chili pepper, to taste
¾ teaspoon of smoked paprika powder

Choka is not so much a dish, but rather a cooking method. Much like stewing is a technique to prepare meat, choka involves roasting vegetables over fire to give them a unique smoky flavor. Baigan is loosely derived from the Hindi word for eggplant. Baigan choka is primarily eaten in Trinidad, typically for breakfast, served alongside a flaky roti. The smoky eggplant pairs wonderfully with creamy tun (another word for polenta) laced with coconut.

INSTRUCTIONS

1. Start by roasting the eggplants: place them over the gas flame of your stove until the exterior is completely charred, turning them halfway through. This process will take approximately 20 to 30 minutes. Do the same with the tomato. If you don't have a gas stove, you can place the eggplants and tomato in the hot coals of a barbecue or roast them in a hot oven for 50 minutes—though you will miss out on the smoky flavor.

2. Meanwhile, preheat the oven to 355°F (175°C). Wrap the unpeeled garlic cloves in aluminum foil and place them in the oven for 15 minutes. When done, they should be completely soft, and you can easily squeeze out the insides.

3. Gently rub off the blackened skin from the eggplants and tomato. Place them with the garlic on a cutting board and chop them into a coarse mixture. Add the ghee, cumin, smoked paprika, and Scotch bonnet, and season with salt and black pepper. Chop and mix thoroughly. Taste and add more salt and pepper if needed. Scoop into a bowl and set aside.

4. For the tun, heat the coconut milk in a medium pan over low heat. Let it simmer for 7 minutes. Then slowly add the polenta, stirring gently. Dissolve the bouillon cube in ¾ cup (200 ml) warm water and add, stirring constantly until you achieve a thick, soft consistency. Lastly, add the cream cheese, Parmesan cheese, mustard powder, and nutmeg. Season with salt and pepper.

5. For the tadka, finely chop the shallot, garlic, and ginger. Heat the ghee for 5 minutes in a small saucepan: the oil must be very hot before you add the rest of the ingredients. Add the shallot, garlic, ginger, rawit or chili pepper, and paprika powder to the pan and cook until the garlic browns, approximately 5 minutes. Ensure the garlic and shallot don't burn; otherwise, the tadka will turn bitter.

6. Scoop the polenta into bowls, top with choka, and finish with a drizzle of the tadka.

The pairing may seem unlikely, but make no mistake: peanuts and bananas, or in this case, plantains, are a match made in culinary heaven. I opt for the blackest plantains I can find; the darker they are, the sweeter they become. Coupled with a salsa made from smoked chili, peanuts, and lime, and topped with crumbled feta, this dish makes a perfect appetizer or a light lunch.

INSTRUCTIONS

1. Preheat your oven to 355°F (175°C) .

2. Place the unpeeled plantains in a baking dish and roast for 20 to 30 minutes, until the skins are black and the insides are completely soft.

3. Slit the roasted plantains lengthwise. Spoon 3 tablespoons of the salsa into each plantain, crumble feta over the top, and serve with a lime wedge on the side.

ROASTED PLANTAINS WITH CHILI-PEANUT-LIME SALSA AND FETA

MAKES 2 SERVINGS

2 plantains, as black as you can find

3 tablespoons of chili-peanut-lime salsa (see p. 217)

~ ⅔ cup (150 grams) of feta

1 lime, cut into wedges

SWEET POTATO PATTIES IN CALLALOO COCONUT SAUCE

MAKES 3-4 SERVINGS

FOR THE SWEET POTATO PATTIES

~ 1¼ cup (270 grams) sweet potato

3 scallions

4 sprigs of thyme

½ teaspoon of cayenne pepper

3 organic limes

~ ⅓ cup (65 grams) of feta

salt and freshly ground black pepper

~ ⅔ cup (150 grams) of coarse polenta

~ ¾ cup (200 ml) of sunflower oil

FOR THE CALLALOO COCONUT SAUCE

2 medium onions

3 cloves of garlic

~ 1 tablespoon (15 grams) chopped ginger

1 Madame Jeanette chili pepper

¼ cup (50 grams) chopped sweet potato leaves (or substitute with spinach)

1 ¾ cup (400 ml) of coconut milk

1 teaspoon brown cane sugar

6 allspice berries

juice of 1 lime

ADDITIONALLY

2 tablespoons of pickled birambi, to serve (see p. 206)

YOU'LL ALSO NEED

a mortar

This vibrant green sauce and vibrant orange vegetarian patties create a colorful feast on your plate. You can easily shape larger or smaller burgers, depending on the appetite of your guests and whether you wish to serve them as a starter or main course. Use plant-based cheese instead of feta for a vegan version.

INSTRUCTIONS

1. Peel the sweet potatoes and cut them into cubes of about ¾-inch. Bring a large pot of water to a boil. Cook the sweet potato until you can easily insert a fork into it, about 15 minutes. Drain and set aside.

2. For the sauce, finely chop the onions, garlic, ginger, and Madame Jeanette chili pepper. Heat the coconut oil in a heavy-bottomed pan. Fry the chopped vegetables until the onion is golden brown. Roughly chop the sweet potato leaves and add them to the pan with the coconut milk, cane sugar, and 1/4 cup (50 ml) water. Let it simmer gently for 10 minutes. Scoop into a blender and blend until smooth. Pour it back into the pan and let it simmer for another 10 minutes on low heat. Grind the allspice berries in a mortar and add to the pan, along with the lime juice.

3. For the patties, slice 1 scallion into rings and set aside. Chop the rest of the scallion finely and put them in a large bowl. Strip the thyme leaves into the bowl. Add the cooked sweet potato, cayenne pepper, grated zest of 2 limes, and the feta, and season with salt and pepper. Mix in ½ cup (100 grams) of the polenta.

4. Form flat balls each using approximately ½ cup (100 grams) from the sweet potato mixture and place them on a baking paper-lined dish or plate. Refrigerate for at least 30 minutes so they hold their shape during frying.

5. Spread 1/4 cup (50 grams) of polenta on a deep plate. Take the patties out of the refrigerator and roll them in the polenta, ensuring they are evenly covered on all sides with a thin layer.

6. Heat the sunflower oil in a frying pan and fry the patties until golden brown on both sides.

7. Cut the remaining lime into wedges. Divide two ladles of the callaloo coconut sauce over deep plates, place a patty on top, and garnish with the reserved scallion, a lime wedge, and some pickled birambi.

This is anything but a traditional recipe. I threw it together on a whim on a winter day, when I still had plantains and a pumpkin that urgently needed to be used. It's a mild, almost sweet curry—if you're a fan of Indian korma, this is really something for you. Feel free to add more chili. I prefer to eat this with a tasty flaky roti.

INSTRUCTIONS

1. Finely chop the onion, garlic, ginger, and Scotch bonnet. Remove the skin from the pumpkin and cut it into ¾-inch cubes. Peel the plantain and cut it into ½ to ¾-inch slices.

2. Heat a large pan over medium heat. Toast the spices for 1 minute or until they start to release their aroma. Add the coconut oil, let it heat up, then add the onion, garlic, ginger, and Scotch bonnet. Fry until the onions become golden brown and start to caramelize.

3. Add the pumpkin, coconut milk, and bay leaves to the pan and let it simmer for 40-50 minutes. Add the plantain and let it simmer for another 20-30 minutes. Season with salt and pepper.

4. Serve with rice or roti and some coconut yogurt and chili flakes on top (see p. 60).

PLANTAIN AND PUMPKIN CURRY

MAKES 4 SERVINGS

2 medium onion

3 cloves of garlic

about 3 tablespoons (20 grams) of ginger, peeled

about 1 teaspoon (3 grams) of Scotch bonnet pepper

2 pounds (1 kilogram, about 4-5 cups chopped) of pumpkin (preferably Kabocha/Japanese pumpkin)

1 plantain

⅛ teaspoon of ground cumin

⅛ teaspoon of cayenne pepper

¼ teaspoon of ground turmeric

1 cinnamon stick

½ teaspoon of yellow mustard seeds

2 teaspoons of Caribbean curry powder (see p. 50)

2 tablespoons of coconut oil

~ 1 ⅔ cups (400 ml) of coconut milk

2 fresh bay leaves

salt and freshly ground black pepper

FISH

This is truly a showstopper, not just because of the colors of the callaloo coconut sauce and the red snapper, but also because of the taste. Your culinary skills will blow your guests away—and they don't need to know that this is actually very easy to make... You can often find fresh red snappers at the fish counter, or otherwise frozen in large Asian supermarkets. Or use dorado. If you can't find fillets, you can ask the fishmonger to fillet a whole fish for you.

INSTRUCTIONS

1. First, prepare the callaloo coconut sauce according to the recipe on page 112.

2. Next, make the cassava purée: peel the cassavas (see p. 34) and cut them into ¾-inch cubes. Place them in a pot with water and bring to a boil. Cook until the cassava falls apart when poked with a fork, which takes about 30 minutes. Drain in a colander and return to the pot. Add the butter, milk, and nutmeg. Mash with a potato masher, then strain over a bowl for a smooth purée. Season with salt and pepper.

3. Salt the fish fillets well on both sides. Heat a bit of oil in a frying pan. When the oil is almost smoking, add the fillets. Flatten them with a spatula to prevent them from curling up. Fry for about 5 to 6 minutes per side until they are golden brown—the exact time depends on the thickness of the fillets. Test by poking a fork in the thickest part: if flakes of fish come off your fork, they are cooked perfectly.

4. Divide the cassava purée among bowls or deep plates and pour the callaloo coconut sauce over it. Carefully place the fillets on the purée, drizzle some thyme oil over them, and top with a few cassava chips.

RED SNAPPER WITH CASSAVA PURÉE, CALLALOO COCONUT SAUCE, AND CASSAVA CHIPS

MAKES 2 SERVINGS

1 recipe for callaloo coconut sauce
(see p. 112)
2 7-ounce (200 grams) red snapper
fillets with skin
coconut oil or other vegetable oil
thyme oil (see p. 60)
1 ½ tablespoons (20 grams)
of cassava chips

FOR THE CASSAVA PURÉE
~ ¾ cup (200 grams) of cassava, pre-peeled
2 tablespoons of salted butter
~ ½ cup (100 ml) of milk
½ teaspoon of freshly grated nutmeg
salt and freshly ground black pepper

YOU'LL ALSO NEED
a potato masher

ESCOVITCH FISH

MAKES 4 SERVINGS

2 whole red snappers, descaled and cleaned
½ teaspoon of allspice berries, plus 4 whole allspice berries
1 teaspoon of smoked paprika
1 teaspoon of cayenne pepper
~ 5 teaspoons (10 grams) of ginger, peeled and finely chopped
juice of 1 lime
salt, to taste
2 cups (500 ml) of vegetable oil
2 sprigs of thyme
2 tablespoons of red lentil flour

FOR THE PICKLE
2 carrots (approximately 4 ounces or 120 grams)
1 large garlic clove
~ 2.5 teaspoons (5 grams) of ginger, peeled
~ 1 teaspoon (5 grams) of Scotch bonnet pepper
1 large onion
½ each of red, yellow, and orange bell peppers
2 tablespoons olive oil
6 sprigs of thyme leaves
4 allspice berries
1 tablespoon of rice vinegar
1 ¾ teaspoons of brown cane sugar
salt and freshly ground black pepper

YOU'LL ALSO NEED
a mortar and pestle
a vegetable peeler
a kitchen thermometer

This dish is the epitome of celebratory fare: a platter of escovitch is always present when there's a celebration in the Caribbean. The supremely crisp fish, lying in full splendor on a beautiful platter, is surrounded by lightly pickled vegetables. It's festive, colorful, and very delicious, causing everyone to dive straight in.

Escovitch derives from the Spanish word "escabeche," meaning fish or meat cooked in vinegar sauce, a technique possibly of Persian origin and later spread around the world by the Spanish. You'll encounter similar recipes in Portuguese, Filipino, and Latin American cultures.

You can usually find red snappers at the fish counter, or otherwise frozen in large Asian supermarkets. Alternatively, you could use mahi-mahi.

INSTRUCTIONS

1. Cut 3 diagonal notches into the sides of the red snappers. Grind the ½ teaspoon of allspice berries in a mortar and mix with the smoked paprika, cayenne pepper, ginger, and lime juice to create a paste. Smear the paste on the inside and outside of the fish. Season generously with salt and place in a large bowl or on a plate. Cover and refrigerate overnight.

2. For the pickle, peel the carrots and then use a vegetable peeler to create thin ribbons. Chop the garlic, ginger, and Scotch bonnet. Slice the onion and bell peppers into thin strips. Heat the olive oil in a frying pan and sauté the onion and garlic until translucent. Add the rest of the vegetables along with the thyme, allspice, Scotch bonnet, vinegar, and sugar. Sauté for 3 to 4 minutes until the vegetables are cooked but still retain some bite. Season with salt and pepper, then remove from the heat and set aside.

3. Heat the oil in a deep frying pan to approximately 340°F (170°C) (use a kitchen thermometer, or dip a piece of bread or the edge of a wooden spoon into the oil: if it immediately bubbles, the oil is hot enough). Place the 4 whole allspice berries and thyme sprigs into the oil; step back, as the oil may splatter.

4. Sprinkle the red lentil flour over the red snappers and fry the fish on both sides for 4 to 5 minutes in the oil. Remove from the pan and let drain on kitchen paper.

5. Serve the fried fish topped with the pickled vegetables. I enjoy eating it with a side of rice, avocado, and fried banana.

CEVICHE

MAKES 2 SERVINGS

1 medium chayote
1 red onion
1 orange
2 limes
1 lemon
2 tablespoons of green seasoning
(see p. 51)
7 ounces (200 grams) of skinless sea
bass fillets
salt and freshly ground black pepper
1 avocado
½ cup or one small handful (20 grams)
of plantain chips

YOU'LL ALSO NEED
a mandoline

Refreshing, tangy, spicy, sweet, creamy, and incredibly easy to prepare, this ceviche might just become your new standard when you have guests over—in which case, you may wish to double or even triple the amounts. Serve as an appetizer or a light main dish on a lovely summer evening. The chayote can be omitted but it does add a pleasingly crunchy texture.

INSTRUCTIONS

1. Slice the chayote and red onion into thin slices using a mandoline and set aside. Remove the peel (including the pith) from the orange, which is easiest if you first cut off the top and bottom. Cut the orange segments away from the membranes and set them aside.

2. Squeeze the juice from the limes and lemon into a bowl and mix with the green seasoning. Cut the sea bass into small cubes and place them in the bowl with the green seasoning-citrus juice. Season generously with salt and pepper and let it marinate for 5 minutes.

3. Remove the skin and pit from the avocado and slice the flesh lengthwise.

4. Divide the fish between two plates and spoon some extra green seasoning-citrus marinade over. Garnish with orange segments, red onion, chayote, avocado, and plantain chips. Serve immediately.

Cassareep, conceived by the original inhabitants of the Caribbean, is a splendid blend of spices and concentrated juice from grated cassava. It works perfectly in stews, particularly in pepperpot, where cassareep forms the secret ingredient (well, not anymore). Cassareep is both sweet and heavily spiced, hence, it seemed to me that it would also work well as a glaze. I was inspired by a recipe from my colleague, Chef Vanja van der Leeden, who glazes mackerel with ketjap manis and serves thin slices of persimmon on the side. This is my version. I prefer to eat the mackerel in a taco, with hot sauce and pickles.

INSTRUCTIONS

1. Ensure all the bones are removed from the mackerel fillets. Grind the smoked salt with the sugar, allspice, and cloves in a coffee grinder or mortar until it forms a fine powder. Sprinkle half of it on a baking dish, place the mackerel fillets on it, and spread the rest of the salt mixture over the fish. Rub the mixture well into the fillets. Let it sit in the fridge for 3 hours.

2. Rinse the fillets under running water. Place them on a plate and pat dry. Brush a layer of cassareep on the skin side of the fillets—if the cassareep is too thick, thin it out with a little hot water.

3. Melt a tablespoon of coconut oil in a frying pan. Wait until the oil sizzles and place the mackerel fillets in the pan, skin side down. Cook for a few minutes on each side. Finish off with another layer of cassareep glaze.

4. Serve with warm tacos, chili sauce, green papaya pickles, and slices of avocado.

CASSAREEP MACKEREL TACOS

MAKES 4 SERVINGS

2 fresh mackerels cut into 4 fillets
2 tablespoons of smoked salt
(or regular salt)
2 tablespoons of brown cane sugar
1 teaspoon of allspice berries
½ teaspoon of cloves
2-3 tablespoons of cassareep (see p. 51)
2 tablespoons of coconut oil
6 corn tortillas
chili sauce, to serve
4 teaspoons of green papaya pickle
(see p. 202)
1 avocado, sliced

YOU'LL ALSO NEED
a coffee grinder or mortar
a brush

SALTFISH

Salting and drying fish to preserve it for long-term use is a process that goes back centuries: without refrigeration, it was, for those not living near the sea or a river, the only way to obtain fish. In the early modern period, trade spread across multiple continents, and salted fish played a significant role in the infamous triangular trade. With bakkeljauw (dried salted cod) from fish from northern seas—and rum, a byproduct of sugarcane—traders bought enslaved Africans, who were also fed the fish on the ships to America and on plantations in the West Indies.

Enslaved individuals and bakkeljauw were so intertwined that their growth paralleled each other. A thriving industry of salted fish developed in Newfoundland in North America, of which almost half was transported to the West Indies.

For centuries, mainly French and Portuguese salt was used to salt fish, but over the course of the seventeenth century, a salt industry emerged in the Caribbean, especially on Bonaire. African slaves worked under abhorrent conditions in the scorching sun on the stark white salt fields, also known as "the white hell."

Thus, the salt went to North America and Northern Europe to salt fish. The salted fish went to Africa where slaves were bought in exchange; and those enslaved were put to work on the salt pans, subsisting on a meager diet that included the very salted fish. It was an endless vicious cycle of oppression.

This is the national pride of Grenada, my father's homeland. My aunts often served the souse for brunch. We would fill the bakes with the souse and large ripe "pears," the Caribbean term for avocados, creating a sandwich.

INSTRUCTIONS

1. Start by preparing the bakes: mix all the dry ingredients in a bowl. Add the butter and use your fingers to create a crumbly dough. While kneading, add about ⅔ cup (150 milliliters) of water. Sprinkle some self-rising flour or regular flour onto a workspace and knead the dough until smooth. Roll it out until it's about 0.8 inches (2 centimeters) thick. Using a glass, cut out 4 to 5 circles of approximately 3 to 3 ½ inches (8 to 9 centimeters) in diameter. Cover them with a damp kitchen towel and let them rest for 30 minutes

2. Place the saltfish in a pot and cover with water. Boil for 20 minutes, using a slotted spoon to remove any salty foam that rises to the surface. Rinse the fish and taste it. It should be salty, but not inedibly so. If it's too salty, put it back in the pot with fresh water and boil for another 5 minutes. Rinse the fish again and set it aside.

3. Dice the bell peppers, scallions, onion, cucumber, Madame Jeanette chili pepper, and tomatoes, then mix them together in a bowl. After allowing it to cool, pull the fish apart with your fingers and add it to the mix. Stir in the coconut oil and season with pepper and, if necessary, a little salt. Heat the oil in a deep pan until it reaches approximately 340°F (170°C) (use a kitchen thermometer or drop a piece of bread or the edge of a wooden spoon into the oil. If it immediately bubbles, the oil is hot enough). Fry the bakes for about 3 minutes on each side, until they are golden brown. Remove from the pan and let drain on paper towels.

4. Slice open the bakes and fill them with the saltfish souse and avocado slices.

SALTFISH SOUSE AND BAKES

MAKES 5 SERVINGS

~ 5 ounces (160 grams) saltfish fillets
½ red bell pepper
½ yellow bell pepper
½ green bell pepper
2 scallions
½ medium white onion
1 mini cucumber
½ Madame Jeanette chili pepper
2 medium tomatoes
1 tablespoon coconut oil
Salt and freshly ground black pepper
1 avocado, sliced

FOR THE BAKES (MAKES 6-7)
2 ½ cups (300 grams) of self-rising flour, plus extra
1 ½ teaspoons of baking powder
¾ teaspoons of salt
¾ teaspoons of granulated sugar
2 ½ tablespoons of butter
1 ⅔ of cups (400 ml) vegetable oil

YOU'LL ALSO NEED
a slotted spoon

The Cuban marinade, mojo, turns any ingredient it encounters into a flavor explosion. Loaded with a profusion of citrus juice, garlic, and herbs, it pairs perfectly with fish, particularly those with a meaty texture such as sea bream. If you can't find sea bream, you can substitute it with other kinds of fish. At the fish counter, ask them to butterfly the fish for you (removing the bone but leaving the skin intact so that the fillets remain connected at the back). This not only makes an impressive presentation but also facilitates eating. Everyone can dig in immediately once you place the fish on the table.

INSTRUCTIONS

1. Ensure that the butterflied fish is entirely clean on the inside, removing any residual blood or organs. Rinse it well. Sprinkle with a few pinches of sea salt, then thoroughly coat it with the mojo. Place it on a plate, cover it with plastic wrap, and let it marinate in the refrigerator for at least 3 hours.

2. Preheat your oven to 450°F (230°C).

3. Place the fish on a baking tray or rack. Put it in the hot oven and bake for 15 minutes. Then, switch the oven to broil and continue cooking for an additional 15 to 20 minutes. This dish is delicious served with the cassava fries found on page 86 or with rice and grilled vegetables.

FISH WITH MOJO

MAKES 2 SERVINGS

1 gilt-head bream or sea bream (approximately 25 ounces or 700 grams), butterflied
Maldon sea salt (or coarse sea salt) to taste
6 tablespoons of mojo (see p. 57)

SALTFISH
AND ACKEE

MAKES 4-5 SERVINGS

5 ½ ounces (150 grams) of saltfish fillets

1 large onion

3 scallions

2 garlic cloves

Half each of a red, green, and yellow
bell pepper

1 or 2 Scotch bonnet peppers (7-10 grams)

3 tablespoons of coconut oil

6 sprigs thyme leaves

2 tomatoes

5 allspice berries

½ teaspoon of coarsely ground
black pepper

½ teaspoon of smoked paprika

19 ounces (540 grams) of canned ackee
(available online)

Salt (optional)

FOR THE BAKES (MAKES 6-7)

2 ½ cups (300 grams) of self-rising flour,
plus extra

1 ½ teaspoons of baking powder

¾ teaspoons of alt

¾ teaspoons of granulated sugar

2 ½ tablespoons of butter

1 ⅔ of cups (400 ml) vegetable oil

As a child, I adored saltfish and ackee for breakfast or brunch, served with fried buns (bakes), fried plantains, and avocado. There was no better breakfast. Saltfish and ackee is one of the most iconic Caribbean dishes, and it's even the national dish of Jamaica. The fruit ackee, brought by enslaved individuals from West Africa, has become the national fruit of Jamaica. It's not very well known outside the Caribbean, and its taste is so unique that I struggle to find an adequate comparison. Visually, it resembles scrambled eggs, but its taste leans more towards creamy avocado—it's truly delectable. Now, you can buy ackee in a can.

INSTRUCTIONS

1. Start by preparing the bakes. Mix all the dry ingredients in a bowl. Add the butter and use your fingers to create a crumbly dough. While kneading, add about ⅔ cup (150 milliliters) of water. Sprinkle some self-rising flour or regular flour onto a workspace and knead the dough until smooth. Roll it out until it's about 0.8 inches (2 centimeters) thick. Using a glass, cut out 4 to 5 circles of approximately 3 to 3 ½ inches (8 to 9 centimeters) in diameter. Cover them with a damp kitchen towel and let them rest for 30 minutes.

2. Place the saltfish in a small pan and cover with water. Boil for 10 minutes. Rinse the fish and taste: it should be salty but not inedibly so. If necessary, set it back in fresh water and boil for a few more minutes. Drain and keep it in fresh cold water.

3. Finely chop the onion, scallions, garlic, bell peppers, and Scotch bonnet. Heat the coconut oil in a frying pan and sauté the chopped vegetables with the thyme until the onions are translucent. Finely chop the tomatoes. Add them to the pan along with the allspice, black pepper, and paprika, and sauté while stirring for 5 minutes.

4. Once cooled to the touch, break up the saltfish with your fingers and add it to the pan. Drain the ackee and add it in as well. Stir very gently: the ackee is quite delicate and breaks apart easily. Taste the sauce to see if it needs more salt. Turn off the heat.

5. Heat the oil in a deep pan until it reaches 340°C (170°C) (Use a kitchen thermometer or drop a piece of bread or the edge of a wooden spoon into the oil. If it immediately bubbles, the oil is hot enough.) Fry the bakes for about 3 minutes on each side, until they are golden brown. Remove from the pan and let drain on paper towels.

6. Cut open the bakes and fill them with the saltfish and ackee.

Green papaya doesn't often make an appearance in Caribbean cuisine, where everyone usually waits for the fruit to ripen. So, when my father mentioned that his Mammy, the woman who cared for him when his parents left for London seeking better work, often made fish with green papaya, I interrupted him to ensure he was remembering correctly. He was certain, including her serving it with a béchamel sauce, a practice that very well could have been a result of the frequent change of colonizers on Grenada, including a stint under French rule.

Instead of a heavy béchamel, I create a sauce with coconut milk. The marriage of salty fish, creamy coconut, and slightly tart green papaya creates an experience that honors the memory of my father's childhood and the unique flavors of Caribbean fusion.

INSTRUCTIONS

1. Finely chop the onion, garlic, Madame Jeanette chili pepper, and ginger. Set aside. Wash the papaya well as you will also use the skin. Cut it widthwise into thin slices, then quarter these slices.

2. Warm the coconut oil in a stew pot over medium heat. Fry the onion, garlic, Madame Jeanette chili pepper, and ginger until the onion is golden brown. Add the sweet potato leaves, coconut milk, sugar, and 2 tablespoons (30 ml) of water and let it simmer for 10 minutes. Transfer the mixture to a blender and process until smooth. Pour it back into the pot, but don't put it back on the heat yet. Add the papaya slices. Grind the allspice in a mortar and pestle and add it to the sauce.

3. Place the saltfish in a small saucepan and cover with water. Bring to a boil and remove any foam that rises to the surface with a slotted spoon. After 20 minutes, remove from heat, rinse, and taste to ensure enough salt has been boiled out. The fish should taste salty, but not excessively so. If it's too salty, boil for another 5 minutes in fresh water.

4. Flake the fish with a fork and add it to the sauce. Place the pot back on the stove and bring the sauce to a boil. Reduce the heat and let it simmer for 50 minutes, or until a fork easily pierces the papaya. Finish with the lime juice and season with salt and pepper to taste.

5. Eat with rice.

SALTFISH IN COCONUT MILK WITH GREEN PAPAYA

MAKES 4 SERVINGS

2 medium onions
3 cloves of garlic
½ Madame Jeanette chili pepper
(or any hot pepper)
½ teaspoon (15 grams) of fresh ginger,
peeled
½ green papaya (approximately
12 ½ ounces or 350 grams)
3 tablespoons of coconut oil
1 ½ ounces (45 grams) of fresh sweet
potato leaves (or substitute with spinach)
1 ⅔ cups (400 ml) of coconut milk
1 teaspoon of brown cane sugar
6 allspice berries
3 ½ ounces (100 grams) of saltfish fillets
juice of 1 lime
salt and freshly ground black pepper

*Freeze the other half, or use it for the
green papaya pickle from page 202

YOU'LL ALSO NEED
a mortar and pestle
a slotted spoon

MEAT

JERK CHICKEN

MAKES 4 SERVINGS

1 whole chicken, about 2.5 pounds
(1.2 kilograms) (or use 8 legs, thighs,
or a mix of them)
1 recipe of jerk marinade (see p. 57)
salt to taste

Jerk chicken, to me, is a mixture of love and irritation. There's no doubting its exquisite flavor and complexity, yet it has become so synonymous with Caribbean food that many people only mention jerk chicken when asked about Caribbean cuisine. It's as if one could encapsulate an entire culinary culture in a single dish. But let's set aside this lament for now and get to preparing this tantalizing dish!

Jerk is not just a marinade but also a method of cooking aimed at preserving meat. This way of salting and smoking meat was invented by Africans who escaped from slavement, Arawaks, and Caribs. Jerk, therefore, has origins in blended cultures and stands as a potent symbol of resistance.

In Jamaica, branches with allspice berries were placed directly into the fire so their aroma would permeate the meat that had been marinated in spices from the Old and New Worlds. I put the allspice directly into the marinade; it works well that way.

INSTRUCTIONS

1. Divide the chicken into 8 pieces. Place the chicken with the breast side down and the legs facing you, then cut them off. This can be done easily by pulling at the joint and cutting through at that point. Next, cut off the wings; when you pull the wing aside, you'll see where it can be cut most easily. With sturdy kitchen scissors or a sharp knife, cut along both sides of the backbone through the ribs. Then cut between the breast to yield two pieces of chicken breast. Go back along the legs to separate the thighs. Save the bones in the refrigerator or freezer for making stock or dispose of them.

2. Place the chicken pieces in a bowl and thoroughly coat them with the marinade and some extra salt. Cover and refrigerate: at least 1 hour, but preferably overnight.

3. Preheat the oven to 400°F (205°C).

4. Place the chicken on a baking sheet, cover with aluminum foil, and bake in the oven for 15 minutes. Remove the foil and return to the oven for an additional 20 minutes.

5. For the true jerk taste, grill the chicken on the barbecue for another 5 minutes, turning frequently.

6. Serve this dish, teeming with the robust flavors of the Caribbean, with freshly made rice and peas (see p. 58) and fried bananas for a complete, satisfying meal.

My father became a phenomenal cook due to his love for food and by learning from the culinary prowess of his mother and sisters. As I was growing up, he was the one who took charge of the kitchen. Before meeting him, my mother was helpless in the kitchen, struggling even with boiling an egg—forgive this public revelation, Mom. I was fascinated by how he could take virtually anything and transform it into something magical. However, one of the best dishes he prepares, which has been improving over the years as he continues to refine the recipe, is his chicken curry. After months of pleading, "Dad, I beg you, write it down," he finally agreed to FaceTime me to dictate his recipe step-by-step. His measurements were just rough estimates. Not a problem, that's where I come in. So, without further ado, here is Conrad's chicken curry.

INSTRUCTIONS

1. Cut the chicken thighs into 4 pieces each. Finely chop the onions and garlic. Peel and cut the sweet potatoes and potatoes into approximately 1-inch (2-centimeter) cubes. Finely chop the Scotch bonnet peppers.

2. Heat the coconut oil in a heavy-bottomed pan, and sauté the curry powder, Scotch bonnet peppers, and sugar until the curry powder is fragrant. Add the onions, garlic, and potatoes, and cook until the onions are translucent. Crumble the bouillon cubes and add them to the pan. Add the chicken to the pan and sauté until all sides are nicely browned. Reduce the heat and add the bay leaves, thyme, vinegar, and approximately 1 cup (200 milliliters) of water. Let it simmer for an hour, then season with salt and black pepper to taste.

3. Serve with either rice or roti (see p. 60).

CONRAD'S CHICKEN CURRY

MAKES 6 SERVINGS

5 chicken thighs (bone-in if you're eating with rice, boneless if eating with roti)
2 onions
4 cloves garlic
~ 1 cup (200 grams) of sweet potatoes
~ ¾ cup (150 grams) of russet potatoes
½ Scotch bonnet pepper
2 tablespoons of coconut oil
2 tablespoons of Caribbean curry powder (see p. 50)
1 teaspoon of brown sugar
2 chicken bouillon cubes
2 bay leaves
4 sprigs of thyme
¾ teaspoon apple cider vinegar
salt and freshly ground black pepper to taste

This chapter is replete with stews and curries that need to simmer slowly and gently on the stove for the most exquisite flavors. Many of these recipes are classics, both within and beyond the Caribbean, and are staples at Caribbean birthdays, christenings, weddings, and funerals.

In Caribbean cuisine, it's customary to eat the whole animal, including the tail, legs, and tougher, muscular parts. Given enough time, these parts transform into super tender, melt-in-your-mouth morsels of meat. Begin in the morning, allowing the delectable aromas to waft throughout your home all day, building anticipation for the evening meal. So take your time, slow down, and wait for the magic to happen.

LOW
& SLOW

CURRY GOAT

MAKES 4 SERVINGS

2 pounds (850 grams) of goat meat
(half with bone, half without)

10 allspice berries

8 tablespoons green seasoning (see p. 51)

Salt and freshly ground black pepper
to taste

1 large white onion

2 scallions

5 cloves garlic

3 tablespoons of coconut oil

3 tablespoons of tomato paste

3 tablespoons of Caribbean curry powder
(see p. 50)

10 sprigs of thyme

1 whole Scotch bonnet pepper

1 ½ cups (300 grams) russet potatoes

YOU'LL ALSO NEED

a mortar and pestle

I distinctly remember the first time I ate curry goat—perhaps it's just as well that no one told me it was goat, or I might not have taken a bite. It was at my father's cousin's wedding, and I sampled some curry from my mother's plate. It was so flavorful, so well-spiced, so juicy, almost sticky. I was hooked. Now that I'm an adult, I prepare goat curry when I want to feel at home—it's the ultimate comfort food. I understand if you're skeptical about goat meat, but when properly prepared, it's one of the most tender meats you'll ever taste. If you can't find goat meat, you can substitute beef brisket or another type of stew meat.

INSTRUCTIONS

1. Ask your butcher to cut the meat into roughly 1.2-inch (3-centimeter) chunks—or do it yourself.

2. Crush the allspice in a mortar. Place the goat meat in a bowl and mix it with the crushed allspice, green seasoning, and a generous amount of salt. Cover and refrigerate overnight.

3. Finely chop the onion, scallions, and garlic.

4. Heat the coconut oil in a large heavy-bottomed pan. Brown the meat on all sides, remove it onto a plate, and set it aside. In the same pan, sauté the onion, scallions, garlic, and tomato paste until the onion is translucent. Stir in the curry powder. Return the meat to the pan, mix well, and add the thyme and Scotch bonnet pepper. Add enough water to cover the meat, reduce the heat, and let it simmer gently.

5. Peel the potatoes and cut them into cubes. After 2 hours and 20 minutes of stewing, add the potatoes to the curry. Continue to stew for another 40 minutes, until the potatoes are cooked and the meat is tender and falling off the bone. Want a thicker curry? Add the potatoes earlier. Season with salt and pepper.

6. Serve with rice and fried plantains.

7. If you have leftover curry goat, pan-fry the remaining meat until it's crispy and serve it with the reheated sauce, coconut tun (see p. 104), pikliz (see p. 205), thyme oil (see p. 60), and cassava chips.

Trini doubles is a popular street food conceived in Trinidad in 1936 by Emamool Deen. Legend has it that the combination of bara (fried bread) with chickpea curry was so irresistible that patrons would always order double portions, hence the name. It's likely inspired by the Indian dish channa bhatura. What I find fascinating about these Caribbean dishes is how clearly their origins can be traced. In this case, it's undoubtedly the Indian contract laborers who came to work on the plantations in Trinidad following the abolition of slavery. They brought with them their fantastic food culture and fused it with Caribbean ingredients such as Scotch bonnet, giving birth to delightful creations like these Trini doubles. I like to serve them with coconut yogurt, tamarind sauce, and cucumber chutney.

INSTRUCTIONS

1. Soak the chickpeas with the baking powder for 24 hours in a bowl of ample water.

2. In a large mixing bowl, combine all the dry ingredients for the baras. Gradually add about 1 cup (220 ml) of lukewarm water while continuously mixing. Dust a work surface or large board with flour and knead the dough until it becomes smooth, approximately 10 minutes. Grease the mixing bowl with coconut oil and return the dough to it. Cover with a damp kitchen towel and set aside for 1 hour to rise. After rising, divide the dough into 10 balls, place them on a large plate or board, and cover them for another hour to let them rise further.

3. In the meantime, skim off the foam from the chickpeas and rinse them under fresh water. Set aside.

4. Finely chop the onion, garlic, and ginger. Heat the coconut oil in a large heavy-bottomed pan over medium heat. Sauté the onion, garlic, and ginger until the onion is golden brown. Add the curry powder, chickpeas, and green seasoning. Stir well, pour in about 1 ¾ cups (400 ml) of water, and let it simmer gently for 40 minutes to 1 hour until you can easily flatten the chickpeas between two fingers. Season with salt and pepper.

5. Prepare the Trini doubles: Heat the sunflower oil in a deep frying pan over medium heat. Stretch each dough ball into a flat circle with a diameter of 4 to 4 ¾ inches (10 to 12 cm). Test if the oil has reached approximately 340°F (170°C) using a kitchen thermometer, or drop a piece of dough into the oil—if it bubbles immediately, the oil is hot enough. Fry each dough circle on both sides for about 3 minutes until golden brown. Remove with a slotted spoon and let it drain on kitchen paper.

6. Serve the curry with the Trini doubles, accompanied by coconut-lime yogurt, cucumber chutney, and tamarind sauce. Enjoy this delightful fusion of Caribbean and Indian flavors, brought to life through the vibrant history of Trinidadian street food.

TRINI DOUBLES

MAKES 6 SERVINGS

FOR THE CHANNA CURRY
1 ¼ cups (250 grams) of dried chickpeas
1 teaspoon of baking powder
1 medium onion
3 cloves garlic
2 teaspoons of peeled and grated ginger
2 tablespoons of coconut oil
2 tablespoon of Caribbean curry powder
(see p. 50)
4 tablespoons of green seasoning
(see p. 51)
salt and freshly ground black pepper

FOR THE BARAS
~ 2 ½ cups (330 grams) of flour,
plus extra
½ teaspoon of baking powder
1 teaspoon of instant yeast
½ teaspoon of ground turmeric
1 teaspoon of salt
2 teaspoons of brown cane sugar
1 tablespoon of coconut oil
1 ¾ cups (400 ml) of sunflower oil
or other vegetable oil, for frying

TO SERVE
coconut-lime yogurt (see p. 223)
cucumber chutney (see p. 213)
tamarind sauce (see p. 213)

YOU'LL ALSO NEED
a frying pan
a kitchen thermometer
a slotted spoon

PEPPERPOT STEW

MAKES 6 SERVINGS

1 pound (350 grams) of brisket

1 pound (500 grams) of oxtail, cut into

1.2-inch (3 cm-) pieces

2 tablespoons green seasoning (see p. 51)

10 sprigs of thyme

3 sprigs of five-in-one herb or 10 sprigs

of oregano

6 whole cloves or ½ teaspoon of ground

cloves

7 allspice berries or ~ 1 teaspoon

of ground allspice

salt and freshly ground black pepper

1 large onion

4 cloves garlic

~ 1 ½ tablespoons (20 grams) of freshly

peeled and grated ginger

1 ½ Scotch bonnet pepper

4 tablespoons coconut oil

½ tablespoon brown sugar

2 (approximately 3-inch) cinnamon sticks

3 tablespoons of cassareep (see p. 51)

1 beef bouillon cube

peel from ½ organic orange

YOU'LL ALSO NEED
a freezer bag
a mortar and pestle

Don't confuse this with pepperpot soup! This rich and flavorful stew includes cassareep, a thick reduction of cassava juice and spices. It originates from Grenada, Guyana, and Barbados, where indigenous cultures longest resisted European colonists, and thus retained more of their culinary traditions than elsewhere. The Arawak would have used bushmeat from the rainforest. I use more easily available meat!

INSTRUCTIONS

1. Cut the brisket into approximately 1 x 1-inch (2 x 2 cm) cubes. Place them in a freezer bag with the oxtail, green seasoning, thyme, five-in-one herb, and cloves. Grind the allspice in a mortar and pestle and add it to the bag along with a generous amount of salt and pepper. Massage the marinade well into the meat. Seal the bag and refrigerate for at least 2 hours, or ideally, overnight.

2. Finely chop the onion, garlic, ginger, and 1 Scotch bonnet pepper (or less if you prefer less heat).

3. Heat the coconut oil in a heavy-bottomed pan and brown the meat on all sides. Once browned, remove the meat and set it aside on a plate.

4. In the same pan, add the onion, garlic, ginger, Scotch bonnet pepper, and sugar, and cook until the onions start to brown. Return the meat to the pan and add enough water to just cover everything.

5. Add the cinnamon sticks, cassareep, bouillon cube, orange peel, and 1 whole Scotch bonnet pepper. Stew the meat for 2 to 2.5 hours until it's completely tender. Taste and adjust the seasoning with more salt and pepper if necessary.

6. Serve this flavorful stew with rice.

CORNBREAD

MAKES 1 LOAF

2 ears of corn

2 small onions

4 scallions

8 tablespoons of butter, plus extra
for greasing

2 ⅓ cups (5000 ml) of milk

¾ teaspoon of lemon juice

1 ½ cups (170 grams) of all-purpose flour

¾ cup (130 grams) of fine cornmeal

¼ cup (50 grams) of coarse cornmeal

2 ½ tablespoons of granulated sugar

3 teaspoons of baking powder

3 teaspoons of salt

2 eggs

3 sprigs of thyme

1 recipe of scallion-jalapeño butter
(see p. 71) to serve

YOU'LL ALSO NEED

a steamer (optional)

8-inch (approximately 20-cm)
springform pan

The array of cornbread recipes is indeed endless. Some call for cornmeal, others for wheat flour, which results in a bread more cake-like in its density. I prefer a combination of the two, crowned with fresh corn kernels that caramelize beautifully with butter and thyme. This bread is perfect for mopping up stews, served alongside fried chicken, or simply enjoyed as is with a generous dollop of jalapeño butter.

INSTRUCTIONS

1. Steam the corn cobs for 20 minutes in a steamer or in a colander placed over a pot of boiling water. Place them on a plate and let them cool.

2. Preheat the oven to 400°F (205°C).

3. Finely chop the onions and scallions. Melt 5 tablespoons of butter in a small pan over low heat until it starts to take on a light brown color. Immediately add the onions and scallions to the pan and sauté over low heat until they become translucent. Be careful not to burn the butter; if it's overheating, remove it from the heat.

4. In a bowl, combine the milk and lemon juice, allowing it to slightly curdle (you could also use buttermilk).

5. In another bowl, mix together the flour, both types of cornmeal, incrementally add the milk, then sugar, baking powder, and salt. Then add the onions along with the butter, and eggs, and mix well.

6. Butter the springform pan.

7. Cut the corn kernels off the cobs and distribute them over the bottom of the pan. Dot with 1 ½ tablespoons (20 grams) of butter, then strip the thyme sprigs and sprinkle the leaves over the top. Pour the batter over the corn and bake for 50 to 60 minutes, or until a knife inserted into the bread comes out clean.

8. Let the bread cool, then remove it from the pan and serve with the scallion-jalapeño butter and a drizzle of honey on each slice.

ROASTED MOJO PORK SHOULDER

I find that slowly braised meat, tender enough to fall apart, is nothing short of heavenly. However, this recipe—deeply spiced with cinnamon and achiote, invigorated by citrus, and fragrantly enhanced by banana leaves—truly shines.

INSTRUCTIONS

1. Begin by brining the pork shoulder. Place the meat in a large bowl, cover with 4 to 8 cups of water, and add the sea salt. Allow it to marinate, covered, in the refrigerator for 24 hours.

2. Remove the meat from the brine and rinse it off. Place it in a bowl and rub the mojo thoroughly over the entire cut. Set it aside.

3. Briefly hold the banana leaves over the open flame of your stove, if you have a gas stove. This will help them release their flavor later on.

4. Preheat the oven to 425°F (220°C).

5. Quarter the onion. Halve the tomatoes and oranges, keeping the skin on. Line the bottom and sides of a large casserole dish with one banana leaf. Place the pork shoulder in the dish, and distribute the onion, tomatoes, oranges, cinnamon, bay leaves, and achiote paste around and on top of it. Season to taste with salt and pepper. Cover with the other banana leaf and a piece of aluminum foil or parchment paper. Place the lid on the dish and put it in the oven for 20 minutes. Then, lower the temperature to 355°F (180°C) and roast for another 2 hours.

6. Remove the dish from the oven and let it rest for a moment. Take off the top banana leaf and shred the meat with two forks. Stir the juice released from the oranges thoroughly into the meat. Season to taste with salt and pepper.

7. Serve, for example, on a tostada (baked tortilla) with pineapple-chili sauce (see p. 218), Trini chow chow (see p. 218), and slices of avocado.

ROASTED MOJO PORK SHOULDER

SERVES 6-8

1 ½ pounds (700 grams) of pork shoulder
1 cup (200 grams) of sea salt
10 tablespoons mojo (see p. 57)
2 large banana leaves, thawed
1 large onion
2 tomatoes
2 organic oranges
2 cinnamon sticks
3 bay leaves
4 tablespoons achiote paste
salt and freshly ground black pepper

OXTAIL STEW

MAKES 4-6 SERVINGS

2 pounds (1 kilogram) oxtail, cut into
1-inch (2 cm) pieces

6 tablespoons green seasoning (see p. 51)

⅛ teaspoon of cayenne pepper

1 tablespoon of ground allspice

salt and freshly ground black pepper

3 tablespoons of coconut oil

2 large onions

1 garlic bulb

~ 1 pound (370 grams) of carrots

1 teaspoon of browning (see p. 50)
or brown cane sugar

1 teaspoon Caribbean curry powder
(see p. 50)

6 teaspoons tomato paste

1 beef bouillon cube

½ teaspoon of Worcestershire sauce

½ cup (60 grams) of flour

1 pound (400 grams) of canned lima
beans (gross weight)

YOU'LL ALSO NEED
a large freezer bag

When I was a child, oxtail was a real treat. My parents worked full time, so dishes that needed to simmer for hours were a rarity. When I got to savor oxtail stew at family parties, I could never get enough, sucking all the juice out of the bones. This is ultimate Caribbean cuisine, particularly adored in Jamaica. The gelatinous oxtail falls apart during the slow-cooking process, becoming incredibly juicy, while the marrow from the bones intensifies the meaty flavor. Perfect for a slow Sunday when you're staying indoors, indulging in the aromas wafting from the kitchen.

INSTRUCTIONS

1. Put the oxtail in a freezer bag with the green seasoning, cayenne pepper, allspice, and a generous pinch of salt. Rub the marinade into the meat well, seal the bag, and refrigerate overnight.

2. Heat 2 tablespoons of coconut oil in a large heavy-bottomed pan. Remove the meat from the bag and brown on all sides. Transfer to a plate.

3. Finely chop the onions and garlic and cut the carrots into large pieces. Fry the onions and garlic in the pan for 2 minutes with the leftover green seasoning from the bag, the browning, and the curry powder. Add the tomato paste and cook for another 2 minutes. Return the meat to the pan, along with the carrots, bouillon cube, and enough water to just cover the meat. Add the Worcestershire sauce, salt, and pepper. Bring to a boil, reduce the heat to low, and let it simmer with the lid on for about 5 hours, or until the meat falls off the bone.

4. After 4-and-a-half hours, prepare the spinners: combine the flour in a bowl with a pinch of salt and 3 tablespoons of water. Knead into a smooth dough on a countertop or board. Take a chunk of dough about the size of a quarter and roll it into an oblong shape in the palm of your hand. Continue making all the spinners in this way and place them on top of the meat. Drain the can of beans and add them to the pan. Let it cook on low heat until the spinners float to the surface.

5. Serve with rice.

LOW & SLOW

Who can resist the allure of fried chicken? Especially when served alongside a creamy carrot curry and sharp carrot pickle, laced with the warmth of ginger. This is a weekend repertoire recipe you'll find yourself coming back to.

INSTRUCTIONS

1. Start by preparing the fried chicken. In a bowl, combine ½ cup (100 ml) milk, ½ teaspoon (2.5 ml) apple cider vinegar, and a generous pinch of salt. Add the chicken, ensuring it's fully submerged in the mixture. Marinate this in the refrigerator for at least an hour, but ideally overnight.

2. To prepare the pickle, peel the carrots and trim off the ends. Use a vegetable peeler to create thin carrot ribbons. In a saucepan, combine ½ cup (120 ml) apple cider vinegar, 2 teaspoons granulated sugar, and ½ teaspoon salt. Grate the ginger directly into the pan. Heat the mixture until the sugar and salt have dissolved and let it cool. Add the carrot ribbons, letting them pickle for anywhere from 30 minutes to an hour.

3. Next, preheat your oven to 350°F (175°C).

4. Now let's make the curry (p. 167). Peel more carrots, trim the ends, halve them lengthwise, and place them in an ovenproof dish. Crush the allspice berries using a mortar and pestle. Mix the olive oil, allspice, paprika, and garlic powder, along with salt and pepper to taste, into the carrots. Roast these in the oven for 20 minutes, or until a fork can easily pierce the carrots.

5. While the carrots are roasting, finely chop the onion, garlic, and Madame Jeanette chili peppers. Grate the ginger and galangal. Heat the coconut oil in a sauté or braising pan and sauté the onion, garlic, peppers, ginger, and galangal until the onions turn translucent. Add the curry powder and sauté until it becomes fragrant. Now, add the roasted carrots, coconut milk, sugar, cinnamon, and bouillon cube, and let it all simmer gently for 30 minutes. Purée with an immersion blender and season with additional salt and pepper to taste

6. Remove the chicken from the milk mixture and place it in a freezer bag with the paprika, cayenne pepper, oregano, garlic powder, chili, and allspice. Ensure the chicken is well coated with the spices.

FRIED CHICKEN WITH CARROT CURRY AND PICKLED CARROT

MAKES 4 SERVINGS

FOR THE FRIED CHICKEN
4 boneless, skinless chicken thighs (about 7 ounces or 200 grams each)
~ ½ cup (100 ml) of milk
¾ teaspoon of apple cider vinegar
salt and freshly ground black pepper
2 teaspoons of smoked paprika
2 teaspoons of cayenne pepper
1 teaspoon of dried oregano
2 teaspoons of garlic powder
½ teaspoon of chili flakes
½ teaspoon of ground allspice
2 eggs
~½ cup (100 grams) of ground red lentils (from an Indian store, or grind yourself, or use regular flour)
1 ⅔ cups (400 ml) sunflower oil or other vegetable oil for frying

FOR THE PICKLED CARROTS
¾ pound (370 grams) of carrots
½ cup (120 ml) of apple cider vinegar
2 teaspoons of granulated sugar
½ teaspoon of salt
1 ½ teaspoon (40 grams) of ginger, peeled

1. Whisk the eggs in a bowl. Place the ground lentils with ample salt and black pepper into another freezer bag or spread out on a plate. Heat the oil in a large pan until it reaches 350°F (175°C) . You can use a cooking thermometer to check the temperature or drop a piece of bread or the edge of a wooden spoon into the oil. If it sizzles immediately, the oil is hot enough. Dip the chicken first in the whisked egg and then coat it with the ground lentils.

2. Fry until golden brown on all sides, which should take around 15 minutes (if you have a cooking thermometer, the internal temperature should reach 165°F or 75°C). Using a slotted spoon, remove the chicken from the pan and let it drain on a paper towel. Next, fry the basil leaves in the oil for just a few seconds, until they become crispy.

3. Serve the fried chicken with the carrot curry, carrot ribbons, and either rice or roti (see p. 60). Garnish with the crispy fried basil leaves and a sprinkle of pink pepper.

FOR THE CARROT CURRY
1 pound (450 grams) of carrots
¼ teaspoon of allspice berries
2 tablespoons of olive oil
¼ teaspoon of paprika
1 teaspoon of garlic powder
salt and freshly ground black pepper
2 small onions
3 cloves of garlic
1 Madame Jeanette chili pepper
1 tablespoon of peeled and grated ginger
1 tablespoon of grated galangal root (available at Asian supermarkets)
1 tablespoon of coconut oil
1 tablespoon of Caribbean curry powder (see p. 50)
1 ⅔ cups (400 ml) of coconut milk
¾ teaspoon of granulated sugar
½ teaspoon of ground cinnamon
½ chicken bouillon cube

ADDITIONALLY
4 sprigs of basil leaves
pinch of freshly ground pink pepper

YOU'LL ALSO NEED
a vegetable peeler
a mortar and pestle
a cooking thermometer
a slotted spoon

PEPPERPOT SOUP WITH SPINNERS

MAKES 6-8 SERVINGS

~ 2 cups (320 grams) of cubed salt meat
~ 2 cups (450 grams) of cubed pork neck
2 scallions
1 large knob of ginger, about 1 inch long (20 grams), peeled
1 vegetable bouillon cube
6 allspice berries
2 shallots
4 cloves of garlic
~ 8 cups (400 grams) of packed sweet potato leaves (or substitute with spinach)
20 small okra pods (~ 9 ounces or 250 grams)
7 sprigs of thyme
~ 1 ½ cups (300 grams) of russet potatoes
~ 1 ¾ cup (400 grams) of purple-skinned sweet potatoes
~ ¾ cup (150 grams) of yam
1 Scotch bonnet pepper
~ ½ cup (60 grams) of flour

On one of the incredibly beautiful white beaches lapped by turquoise sea of Carriacou island, a part of Grenada, lies the Callaloo restaurant. This place is famous for its callaloo soup, a simpler version of the pepperpot soup, but with the same green leafy vegetables as a base. The pepperpot soup also contains salted meat and okra, which together create a unique taste experience.

INSTRUCTIONS

1. Cut the salt meat into cubes of about ½ inch and place in a small pan covered with cold water. Bring it to a boil. Once it starts boiling, drain the water and place the meat in fresh cold water.

2. Cut the pork neck into cubes of about 1 inch and place them in a large pot. Coarsely chop the scallions, ginger, and the bouillon cube. Add approximately ¾ gallon (3 liters) of water, the drained salt meat, and the allspice. Simmer gently until the meat is tender, which should take 1 to 2 hours.

3. Coarsely chop the shallots and garlic. Remove the cooked meat from the pot and set it aside. Add the garlic, shallots, sweet potato leaves, and okra to the pot. Strip the leaves from the thyme sprigs and add them in. Cook for 5 to 10 minutes until the okra is soft.

4. Peel the potato, sweet potato, and yam and cut them into cubes of about ½ inch (1 centimeter).

5. Purée the soup with an immersion blender. Add the potato, sweet potato, yam, and whole Scotch bonnet pepper to the pot and cook for another 20 minutes.

6. Meanwhile, make the spinners: in a bowl, combine the flour with a pinch of salt and 3 tablespoons (45 ml) of water. Knead on a work surface or cutting board until the dough is smooth. Take a piece of dough about the size of a quarter and roll it in the palm of your hand into an elongated shape. Repeat this process to create all of the spinners. Add them to the soup and cook with the lid on for 30 minutes.

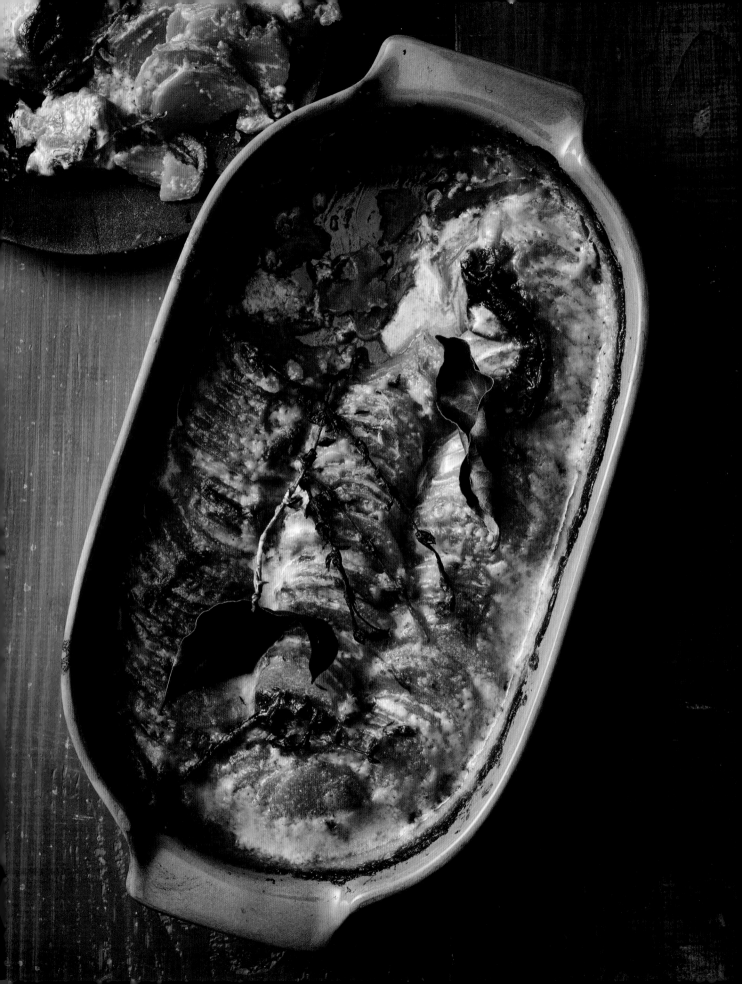

This recipe was conceived on a whim, I must confess. On Sundays, I yearn for comfort food, for dishes that have spent a long time simmering on the stove or baking in the oven—a tradition I inherited from home. My favorites are roast leg of lamb or braised oxtail. Usually, I pair these with roasted potatoes or rice and peas, but sometimes I crave something different. That's how this oven gratin came about. The sweet potatoes caramelize beautifully and become delightfully chewy, with the ginger adding a welcome kick. Don't just walk to cook this one, RUN!

INSTRUCTIONS

1. Preheat the oven to 355°F (175°C).

2. Peel the sweet potatoes. Set the mandoline slicer to a fine setting and cut the potatoes into very thin slices. Arrange the slices upright in rows in a baking dish.

3. Pour the cream into a small saucepan and place it over low heat. Grate the ginger and garlic and add them to the cream, along with the thyme leaves, bay leaves, and chili flakes. Crumble the bouillon cube over the cream. Allow the cream to gently simmer for about 10 minutes. Season generously with black pepper and a little salt. Pour the cream over the sweet potatoes and cover the dish with aluminum foil.

4. Bake in the oven for approximately 40 minutes. Remove the foil and return the potatoes to the oven for another 10 to 15 minutes.

SWEET POTATO GRATIN WITH GINGER CREAM

MAKES 4-6 SERVINGS

2 large or 3 medium sweet potatoes (850 grams)
1 ¼ cups (300 ml) of (coconut) cream (or high-fat coconut milk)
1 ½ tablespoons of ginger, peeled
2 cloves of garlic
5 sprigs of thyme, stripped of leaves
2 bay leaves
½ teaspoon of chili flakes
1 vegetable bouillon cube
salt and freshly ground black pepper

YOU'LL ALSO NEED
a mandoline slicer

I have an immense sweet tooth and I must marshal all my willpower to keep myself from stuffing every piece of sugar and candy I encounter into my mouth. It seems that Caribbean people share this condition, or enthusiasm—it all depends on your perspective. This is somewhat ironic, given that sugar has been the cause of so much suffering in the Caribbean for centuries. Yet, as with many of the tragedies that occurred on the islands, the residents turned things around and, over time, used sugar to concoct colorful confectioneries of all sorts, fabulous cakes, and sweet drinks. This chapter may not contain many traditional sweets, but it does feature new creations and classics with Caribbean ingredients.

SWEET TREATS

TRES LECHES

MAKES 6-8 SERVINGS

2 cups (230 grams) of flour

¾ teaspoon of baking powder

pinch of salt

5 eggs

¾ cup (150 grams) of white caster (super fine) sugar

2 teaspoons of vanilla extract

1 tablespoon of butter

½ cup (150 ml) of whole milk

½ cup (150 ml) of evaporated milk

4 tablespoons of condensed coconut milk

2 ½ cups (600 ml) of heavy cream

4 tablespoons of powdered sugar

½ teaspoon of ground cinnamon

zest of 1 organic orange

YOU'LL ALSO NEED
a baking dish approximately
16 x 11 inches (40 x 28 cm)

This cake is one of my favorite dishes. I first tasted it in a Venezuelan restaurant in the Crystal Palace neighborhood of South London, and I was astounded by the similarities between the cuisine of the Caribbean islands and this South American country. If you love tiramisu, you'll certainly appreciate tres leches cake. The cake is extremely fluffy, almost like angel cake, soaked in three types of milk, with subtle flavors of vanilla and coconut. Truly heavenly. Top it off with whipped cream, cinnamon, and orange zest—it's hard not to eat the whole cake in one go!

INSTRUCTIONS

1. Preheat the oven to 335°F (168°C).

2. Mix the flour, baking powder, and a pinch of salt in a large mixing bowl. Separate the eggs. Using a handheld mixer, beat the yolks with about 4 ½ tablespoons (75 grams) of caster (super fine) sugar until they turn pale yellow. Sift the flour mixture into the bowl and combine thoroughly.

3. Clean a bowl, a whisk, or the mixer beaters and your hands properly—if any fat gets into the egg whites, you won't be able to whip them to peaks. Yolks also contain fat, so be careful. Whisk the egg whites until soft peaks form. Add the remaining 4 ½ tablespoons (75 grams) of sugar and 1 teaspoon of vanilla extract, and beat until you get firm, glossy peaks. Gently fold this into the flour-egg yolk mixture.

4. Grease a baking dish with butter. Pour the batter into it and bake for 20 to 25 minutes, or until a fork inserted into the cake comes out clean.

5. Meanwhile, in a bowl, combine ½ cup (150 ml) of whole milk, ½ cup (150 ml) of evaporated milk, and 4 tablespoons of condensed coconut milk with 1 teaspoon of vanilla extract. In another bowl, beat 2 ½ cups (600 ml) of heavy cream with 4 tablespoons (60 grams) of powdered sugar until it thickens.

6. Allow the cake to cool slightly. Using a skewer or fork, poke holes in the cake and pour the milk mixture over it. Spread the thickened cream on top and sprinkle with cinnamon and orange zest.

In my childhood, my mother held a particular affection for crème brûlée, a sentiment I believe lingered in my mind as I dreamed up this recipe. I chose to imbue it with a tropical spin, incorporating corn into the custard—or, to speak in more elegant terms: crème anglaise—and adorning it with a caramelized topping of guava. The end result is a harmonious balance between fruity and earthy flavors.

INSTRUCTIONS

1. Preheat the oven to 325°F (162°C).

2. Pour the crème anglaise into ramekins, covering each with aluminum foil. Place them in a high-sided baking dish and fill it with boiling water until the ramekins are halfway submerged. Bake for 30 to 45 minutes until the crème has set at the edges but remains jiggly in the middle.

3. Meanwhile, combine the guava paste and sugar in a food processor until well mixed.

4. Remove the crème anglaise from the oven and allow it to cool slightly. Sprinkle the guava sugar across the top. Using a crème brûlée torch, caramelize the sugar until it bubbles and takes on a light brown hue. Don't have a torch? Position it briefly under the broiler.

CORN CRÈME BRÛLÉE WITH GUAVA

MAKES TWO SERVINGS

6 tablespoons of maize crème anglaise (see recipe for maize crème anglaise, p. 195)
7 tablespoons of guava paste
1 tablespoon of white caster (super fine) sugar

YOU'LL ALSO NEED
two ramekins
crème brûlée torch

SUGAR

Few products boast such a tumultuous and dark history as sugar. It brought immeasurable changes to the Caribbean, in economic, agricultural, social, and political terms. And not only the Caribbean—sugar has prompted a vast shift in the world's culinary landscape. The insatiable European sweet tooth was a key reason millions of Africans were enslaved. This is not dissimilar to the fast fashion industry, which forces millions to labor under exploitative, inhumane conditions, just so we can revamp our wardrobes each month.

The origins of sugarcane, a grass that sprouts thick fibrous stalks reaching up to twenty feet or six meters high, are in New Guinea, where the crop was domesticated ten thousand years ago. By the sixth century, it had found its way to India, where they discovered how to extract juice from the cane, convert it into molasses, and subsequently sugar crystals (khanda in Sanskrit—possibly the origin of the word "candy"). Arab traders introduced sugar to Southern Europe in the Middle Ages. Frustrated by the Arab monopoly, Europeans attempted to grow their own sugarcane, first on Madeira and later on the Canary Islands. This led to the creation of the plantation system, where cheap or free labor was used on large swaths of land to cultivate profitable crops—African slaves had already worked on sugar plantations on Madeira and the Canary Islands before the trans-Atlantic trade began.

On Columbus' second voyage, he brought sugarcane to the Caribbean. Thus, the dark history of sugar grew even darker. From the seventeenth century, enslaved Africans labored on sugarcane plantations on the islands. In total, around five million Africans were brought to the Caribbean, nearly half to the British Caribbean. To process sugar into an edible product, enslaved Africans worked day and night cutting, crushing, and cooking the cane. No one was spared: the sick, pregnant women, the elderly, and the weak were all forced to work endlessly.

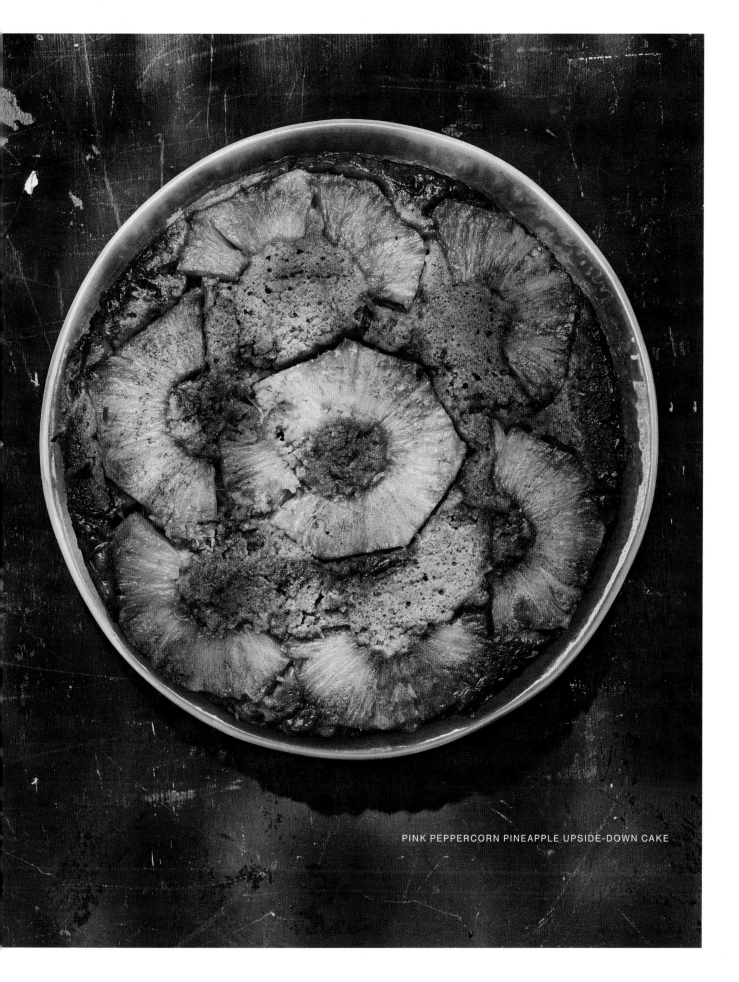

PINK PEPPERCORN PINEAPPLE UPSIDE-DOWN CAKE

PINK PEPPERCORN PINEAPPLE UPSIDE-DOWN CAKE

MAKES 6-8 SERVINGS

FOR THE CARAMEL
1 stick plus 1 tablespoon (250 = grams) butter, plus extra for greasing
½ cup plus 2 tablespoons (250 grams) dark brown sugar
4 green cardamom pods
4 tablespoons dark rum

FOR THE CAKE BATTER
8 green cardamom pods (or ¾ of a teaspoon of ground cardamom)
20 pink peppercorns
3 cups plus 2 tablespoons (400 grams) flour
2 teaspoons of baking powder
14 tablespoons (200 grams) of salted butter
1 cup (200 grams) of dark brown sugar
2 teaspoons of vanilla extract
3 large eggs
⅔ cup (270 grams) of Greek yogurt
½ cup 20 ml) of sunflower oil

ADDITIONALLY
2 medium pineapples
1 recipe coconut mascarpone (see p.194)

YOU'LL ALSO NEED
a mandolin
12 muffin cups
9.5-inch (24 cm) (approximately) springform pan
a mortar and pestle

This recipe offers an elegant twist on the classic pineapple upside-down cake, a dessert that's been made and reimagined for decades. The basic concept is simple: pour cake batter over slices of fruit and flip the cake after baking to reveal a beautifully caramelized layer of fruit—in this case, pineapple. The batter in this version is uplifted with the addition of pink peppercorns and cardamom.

INSTRUCTIONS

1. Begin by creating "pineapple flowers" for decoration: Preheat the oven to 215°F (100°C). Peel one pineapple but leave the hard core intact. Using a mandolin or sharp knife, slice the pineapple into the thinnest possible cross-sections. Pat the slices dry with kitchen paper. Lay them on a baking sheet lined with parchment paper and bake for 50 minutes, so they begin to dry. Flip the slices and return them to the oven for another 50 minutes. Drying times may vary; they are ready when the slices can be easily snapped between your fingers. Press them into muffin cups, forming them into a flower shape. Place them on a plate and leave to dry overnight in a cool, dry place (not the refrigerator, as they will soften).

2. For the cake, preheat the oven to 350°F (175°C).

3. Remove the skin and any brown spots from the second pineapple. Cut away the hard core without damaging the flesh (as if you were coring an apple) and slice the fruit lengthwise into ¾-inch (2 cm) slices.

4. Prepare the caramel: Warm the butter, sugar, cardamom pods, and rum in a small pan over low to medium heat. Let it gently simmer until it starts to bubble. Meanwhile, grease a springform pan with butter. Remove the cardamom pods from the caramel with a fork, then pour the hot caramel over the bottom of the pan. Arrange the pineapple slices in a single layer over the caramel.

5. In a mortar, bruise 4 cardamom pods and extract the seeds. Discard the pods. Grind the seeds with the pink peppercorns until finely powdered.

6. Mix the flour and baking powder in a bowl. In a separate bowl, whip the butter, sugar, and vanilla extract with a hand mixer until fluffy. Mix in the eggs. Gradually add the flour while continuing to mix. Next, add the Greek yogurt and then the sunflower oil. Stir in the pink pepper, cardamom, and a pinch of salt at the very end. Pour the batter over the pineapple and bake for 45-50 minutes. Check if the cake is ready by inserting a toothpick or fork; if it comes out clean, the cake is done. Allow it to cool for 10-15 minutes, then flip it onto a cooling rack and remove the springform pan.

7. If you are feeling extra you can make another batch of the caramel to drizzle on top.

8. Once the cake has completely cooled, serve the coconut mascarpone Drizzle with the extra caramel and decorate with the pineapple flowers to serve an elegant and refreshing dessert sure to impress.

I was enamored with sweet potato pudding as a child, attracted by its sweet, nutty flavor, and soft, sticky texture. The brown butter in this version makes it even stickier, and chewy around the edges. Savor this spiced pudding fresh out of the oven with a scoop of vanilla ice cream, and you'll find yourself in dessert heaven.

INSTRUCTIONS

1. Preheat the oven to 350°F (175°C).

2. Place the whole sweet potatoes in a baking dish and roast for 40 minutes, or until you can easily pierce them with a fork. Allow them to cool but keep the oven on.

3. Cut the sweet potatoes open and scoop the soft flesh into a large bowl. Mash it with a potato masher—it doesn't need to be perfectly smooth.

4. In a saucepan over low heat, melt the butter with the cinnamon stick until small brown flakes appear and the butter turns a hazelnut brown color. Turn off the heat and remove the cinnamon.

5. Add the coconut powder, the flour, brown sugar, ginger, nutmeg, vanilla, lime juice, brown butter, and salt to the mashed sweet potatoes. Mix thoroughly.

6. Grease a baking dish with some butter and pour the mixture into it. Bake for 1 hour in the preheated oven until the top is golden brown and the pudding is still slightly jiggly in the center when you gently shake the baking dish. It will firm up as it cools.

7. Serve warm, with a scoop of vanilla ice cream on top.

BROWN BUTTER SWEET POTATO PUDDING

MAKES 6 SERVINGS

2 ½ pounds (1 kg) of purple sweet potatoes
7 tablespoons (100 grams or slightly less than a stick) butter, plus extra for greasing
1 cinnamon stick
⅓ cup (30 grams) coconut powder
½ cup plus 1 tablespoon (70 grams) all-purpose flour
¾ cup (150 grams) of dark brown sugar
1 teaspoon of grated ginger
½ teaspoon of freshly grated nutmeg
½ teaspoon of vanilla extract
juice of ½ lime
2 pinches of salt
vanilla ice cream, to serve

YOU'LL ALSO NEED
a potato masher
a baking dish approximately 15 by 11 inches (38 by 28 cm)

A true showstopper. Trust me, after it's all over, you'll be glad you pulled out all the stops. Your guests will be, too, assuming you're generous enough to share a piece with them... As a child, I couldn't get enough of Eton mess—a delightful mix of broken meringue pieces, whipped cream, fruit, and fruit coulis. This pavlova pays homage to that, with a tropical twist. The airy whipped mascarpone contrasts nicely with the tangy passion fruit and sweet meringue.

INSTRUCTIONS

1. Preheat the oven to 250°F (120°C).

2. Thoroughly wash a bowl, a whisk, and your hands—if the egg whites come into contact with fat, they won't whip up. Be especially careful with the egg yolks, which also contain fat. Whip the egg whites with the cornstarch, lemon juice, and vanilla until soft peaks form. Gradually add the sugar while continuing to whip until the mixture holds stiff, shiny peaks.

3. Place a plate on a piece of parchment paper and trace the outline. Spread the meringue within this circle. Use a rubber spatula to smooth the top, ensuring the edges are higher to beautifully contain the filling later. Bake the meringue in the oven for 1 hour, then turn off the oven and allow it to slowly cool inside for another hour.

4. While the meringue is cooling, prepare the curd. Scoop the pulp from 4 passion fruits and combine with the lemon and lime juices and the sugar in a pan. Warm over low to medium heat until the sugar has dissolved. Beat the egg yolks in a separate bowl. Gradually add them to the pan, stirring continuously, making sure that nothing sticks to the bottom of the pan. After about 20 minutes of stirring, the mixture should have thickened nicely—it's ready when it clings to the back of a spoon. Turn off the heat and stir in the butter until it has melted. Allow the curd to cool, then store it in a sterilized jar in the refrigerator for up to 1 month.

5. In a separate bowl, whip together the mascarpone and milk.

6. Carefully lift the cooled meringue from the parchment paper and place it on a serving dish. Spread the whipped mascarpone over the top. Generously dollop passion fruit curd on top. Scoop the pulp from the remaining 2 passion fruits onto the Pavlova and garnish with a few mint leaves. Enjoy!

PAVLOVA WITH PASSION FRUIT CURD AND WHIPPED MASCARPONE

MAKES 6 SERVINGS

FOR THE PAVLOVA
4 egg whites
1 teaspoon of cornstarch
1 teaspoon of lemon juice
1 teaspoon of vanilla extract
¾ cup (150 grams) of caster (super fine) sugar

FOR THE PASSION FRUIT CURD
6 passion fruits
2 tablespoons of lemon juice
2 tablespoons of lime juice
⅓ cup (70 grams) of granulated sugar
3 egg yolks
5 tablespoons of salted butter

FOR THE WHIPPED MASCARPONE
3 tablespoons of mascarpone
3 tablespoons of milk

TO GARNISH
a handful of fresh mint leaves

YOU'LL ALSO NEED
a sterilized jar of approximately ¾ cup (150 ml) capacity (see p. 200)

CHOCOLATE AVOCADO MOUSSE

MAKES 4-6 SERVINGS

5 ½ ounces (160 grams) of dark
chocolate, chopped

3 avocados, ripe

1 ½ tablespoon of cocoa powder

2 tablespoons of agave syrup

zest of 2 organic mandarins

1 teaspoon of condensed coconut milk
(or regular condensed milk)

3 teaspoons of vanilla extract

a pinch of Maldon salt (or coarse sea salt)

Avocado might not be the first thing that comes to mind when thinking about desserts, but technically it's a fruit—and we do often incorporate fruit into our desserts. So, why not? Choose the creamiest avocado you can find, and half the work is already done.

INSTRUCTIONS

1. Melt the chocolate using a double boiler by placing a glass bowl over a small saucepan filled with water—just ensure the water doesn't touch the bottom of the bowl. Bring the water to a simmer over medium heat, add the chocolate to the bowl, and stir until it has melted. Remove the bowl from the heat and let it cool slightly.

2. Remove the pits from the avocados and scoop the flesh into a food processor. Add the melted chocolate and all other ingredients except the salt. Blend until well mixed and then strain the mixture over a bowl.

3. Stir in a generous pinch of Maldon salt (or coarse sea salt) at the end. Serve as is, or to enhance the flavor, consider adding a splash of corn crème anglaise (see p. 195), plantain chips, or homemade ginger crumble.

FOR THE GINGER CRUMBLE
3 McVitie's Ginger Nuts (or digestive biscuits)
2 teaspoons (10 grams) ginger, peeled

Preheat the oven to 350°F (175°C). Grate the ginger. Combine it with the biscuits in a food processor and pulse until you have a fine crumble. Line a baking dish with parchment paper and spread the crumble evenly over it. Bake for 10 to 15 minutes. Remove from the oven and let it cool. Crumble it again and use it immediately.

PANCAKES WITH COCONUT MASCARPONE AND PLANTAIN IN CARDAMOM BUTTERSCOTCH

MAKES 4-6 SERVINGS

1 ripe, almost black, plantain
~ ¼ cup (60 ml) of coconut oil, plus extra

FOR THE CARDAMOM BUTTERSCOTCH
4 green cardamom pods
4 tablespoons of butter
~ 2 tablespoons (25 g) of granulated sugar

FOR THE PANCAKES
1 ½ cups (180 g) of all-purpose flour
1 ½ tablespoons of granulated sugar
1 ½ teaspoons of baking powder
⅛ teaspoon of ground cinnamon
2 eggs
1 ¼ cups (300 ml) milk (oat milk can also be used)
¼ teaspoon of vanilla extract
¾ teaspoon of salt

FOR THE COCONUT MASCARPONE
~ ½ cup (15 g) of dried grated coconut
~ ½ cup (100 g) of mascarpone
~ 2 tablespoons (25 g) of powdered sugar
1 vanilla bean
a pinch of salt

YOU'LL ALSO NEED
a mortar and pestle

In Caribbean cuisine, we consume plantains in copious amounts. The longer they ripen, the sweeter they become—this is evident in the dark, nearly black color of the skin. Think of the words of rapper Tupac Shakur: "The blacker the berry, the sweeter the juice." This analogy is particularly fitting when you consider that bananas are technically berries. They continue to ripen, so if you can't find black plantains, simply let them sit for a few days until they acquire the desired color.

INSTRUCTIONS

1. First, make the butterscotch: Crush the cardamom in a mortar and pestle, remove the seeds, and grind them into a fine powder. Melt the butter in a frying pan over low heat. Add the sugar and stir until it is dissolved. Add the cardamom, stir to combine, then add approximately ¼ cup (50 ml) of water. Allow the mixture to simmer gently until it thickens, about 10 to 15 minutes. Set aside.

2. For the pancakes, combine all the dry ingredients in a bowl. Add the eggs, milk, vanilla extract, and salt and mix well. It's okay if there are still some lumps in the batter; this will make the pancakes fluffier. Set aside.

3. To prepare the coconut mascarpone, heat a frying pan over low to medium heat. Once the pan is hot, toast the coconut until it begins to brown and emit a pleasing aroma. Remove immediately from the heat to prevent burning. In a bowl, mix the toasted coconut with the mascarpone and powdered sugar. Split the vanilla bean lengthwise and scrape out the seeds. Add the seeds and a pinch of salt to the mascarpone mixture. Stir well and set aside.

4. Peel the plantain and cut it into diagonal slices about ½ inch (1 cm) thick. Heat a frying pan over medium heat. Warm 4 tablespoons of coconut oil until it begins to sizzle. Fry the plantain slices in the oil until both sides are brown and slightly crispy. Place the slices in the butterscotch and warm over low heat, ensuring the slices are well coated with the sauce.

5. Cook the pancakes: Heat a frying pan over medium heat. Add 1 teaspoon of coconut oil and wait until it begins to sizzle. Pour half a ladle of pancake batter into the pan. Cook for about 2 minutes on each side, until golden brown. Continue this process until all the batter is used up. Keep the cooked pancakes on a plate covered with aluminum foil to keep them warm.

6. To serve, stack the pancakes on each plate, add a few slices of plantain, drizzle with additional butterscotch, and top with a tablespoon of coconut mascarpone.

When Europeans first arrived in the New World and tasted corn, they were unimpressed, deeming corn unsuitable for human consumption and using it only as fodder. Contrastingly, in the indigenous cultures, corn had been cultivated for thousands of years. Corn was a mainstay at religious ceremonies, even offered as sacrifice to the gods. Today, corn is among the top three most cultivated crops globally.

Usually, corn is used in savory dishes, but here we explore its sweet side. Inspired by a vegetarian restaurant called Bak in Amsterdam, where their corn ice cream completely blew me away, I wanted to create something similar that brings out the earthy and sweet taste of corn. Enjoy the crème anglaise as is, or with a dish that would traditionally be served with crème anglaise. I have also created a baked version topped with caramelized guava and sugar, which can be found on page 181.

INSTRUCTIONS

1. Steam the corn for about 20 minutes in a steamer or in a colander placed over a pan of boiling water. Let it cool slightly.

2. Stand each cob vertically on a board and cut off the corn kernels. Blend the corn in a food processor until smooth. Sieve the mixture into a bowl, making sure to scrape off the bottom of the sieve with a rubber spatula.

3. In a bowl, whisk together the egg yolks and sugar with a fork.

4. Pour the milk and cream into a saucepan. Split the vanilla pod lengthwise and scrape out the seeds with a knife. Add the seeds and the pod to the pan. Simmer on low heat for 15 minutes without boiling. Gradually whisk the hot mixture into the egg-sugar mixture, then return it to the pan along with the corn and simmer on low heat. Keep whisking until you have a thick crème that clings to a spoon.

5. Enjoy it with one of the cakes from this book or serve it cold with the chocolate avocado mousse from page 190 on top.

MAIZE CRÈME ANGLAISE

MAKES 2-4 SERVINGS

4 medium-size corn cobs
3 large egg yolks
2 ½ tablespoons of white caster (super fine) sugar
~ ½ cup (100 ml) of whole milk
~ ½ cup (100 ml) of whipping cream
1 vanilla pod (or 1 teaspoon of pure vanilla extract as a substitute)

YOU'LL ALSO NEED
a steamer (optional)

Shave ice vendors can be found on nearly every street corner and all markets in the Caribbean islands, offering a plethora of flavors. I was delighted when I found a shaved ice cart in the summer wandering around the Amsterdam Dappermarkt. I always go for maracuja, as they call passion fruit on the French-speaking Caribbean islands—the word comes from the Portuguese via the Tupi. This granita is an easy home version, made without big ice blocks or special ice shavers.

INSTRUCTIONS

1. Combine 4 tablespoons of sugar with ¾ cup (180 milliliters) of water in a small saucepan and heat over medium heat until the sugar has dissolved. Allow it to cool completely.

2. Halve the passion fruits and scoop the pulp into a bowl, add the zest and juice of the mandarin. Add the sugar water and mix well. Pour into a large dish or container and freeze for 45 minutes. Scrape with a fork to form small crystals. Freeze for an additional hour and repeat the scraping. Freeze for one more hour.

3. Meanwhile, remove the skin from the orange, including the white pith, and cut the fruit out into segments. Combine in a bowl with the remaining sugar, the grated rind, and the juice of both the lemon and lime.

4. Place a few orange segments on plates and scoop the granita on top. Finish with a spoonful of condensed milk. This delightful dessert will transport your taste buds to the Caribbean. Enjoy!

PASSION FRUIT GRANITA

MAKES 2-3 SERVINGS.

6 tablespoons of white caster (super fine) sugar
9 passion fruits
1 organic mandarin
1 orange
1 organic lemon
1 organic lime
2-3 tablespoons of condensed milk

As you flip through this book, you might notice a great assortment of recipes devoted to condiments. This isn't an accident. I have an immense fondness for condiments, something that is quite evident by the top shelf, and slowly but surely, the one below it in my refrigerator, being packed with jars of sauces and pickles. I frequently utilize them as they readily add an extra dimension of flavor to soups, stews, or curries. Alternatively, I serve them alongside a dish where, sometimes, a sauce or a pickle lends the precise balance of spiciness or acidity needed in your mouth.

The people of the Caribbean islands share my fondness for condiments. Almost every island boasts its own array of hot sauces and pickled fruits and vegetables. From Barbados hot pepper sauce with mustard to cucumber chutney adding a delightful crunch to Trini doubles (see p. 153). There's so much more to discover. Pickles and condiments play a vital role in many recipes in this book. It's important to have a sterilized bottle or jar to ensure that the sauce, drink, or pickle remains fresh for longer.

PICKLES & SAUCES

STERILIZATION

I usually opt for a quick method of sterilization.
I pour boiling water into freshly washed jars and
bottles, swish it around to ensure it covers all areas,
drain the water, and let them dry and cool on a clean
tea towel. Want a more thorough approach? Have the
jars and bottles run through a hot cycle in the
dishwasher or boil them for 15 minutes in a pan of
boiling water. Alternatively, you can put them in a
210°F (99°C) oven for 15 minutes.

GREEN PAPAYA PICKLE

MAKES APPROXIMATELY 3 CUPS (700 ML)

~1 ½ to 2 cups (275 grams) of prepared
green papaya (peeled and seeds
removed)
¾ cup (150 ml) apple cider vinegar
⅔ cup (80 grams) granulated sugar
6 whole cloves
6 juniper berries
1 teaspoon yellow mustard seeds
¾ teaspoon salt
~2 tablespoons (10 grams) of peeled and
grated or finely chopped ginger
1 Madame Jeanette chili pepper
1 organic lime (only the zest will be used)

YOU'LL ALSO NEED
2 sterilized jars of approximately
1 ½ cups (340 ml) each (see p. 200).
Cool before filling.)

As I've written before, we don't often use green, unripe papaya in the Caribbean. This is a shame, as unripe papaya is very versatile, something Asia is well aware of. This recipe was inspired by a friend who introduced me to Japanese green papaya pickle. Thank you, Akane!

INSTRUCTIONS

1. Thoroughly wash the green papaya since we'll be using it with the skin. Halve it and scoop out the seeds with a spoon. Dice one half of the papaya and set aside. (Use the other half for the callaloo fish stew, see p. 121.)

2. Now, let's prepare the brine: gently warm the vinegar and ¾ cup (170 ml) water in a small saucepan over low heat. Add the sugar, cloves, juniper berries, mustard seeds, and salt, letting it simmer until the sugar and salt have dissolved.

3. In the meantime, slice the ginger and halve the Madame Jeanette chili pepper lengthwise. Zest the lime and cut it into small pieces.

4. In the jars, layer the papaya, ginger, Madame Jeanette chili pepper, and lime zest. Pour the brine over it.

5. Store in the refrigerator. The pickle is ready after one month and can be kept for up to three months thereafter.

Pikliz is a standard staple in every Haitian household. Exceptionally easy to make and versatile, it's perfect for tacos, roast meats, fried fish, sandwiches, roasted vegetables, and so on. Inexpensive and straightforward, Pikliz is something you'll always want to have in your refrigerator.

INSTRUCTIONS

1. Using a mandoline, slice the cabbage into thin strips and cut the carrot into thin batons. Slice the shallot lengthwise into thin slices and finely chop the Scotch bonnet peppers. Place all the ingredients into a bowl and mix well. Season to taste with salt and pepper.

2. Transfer the Pikliz into a sterilized jar and store it in the refrigerator for up to 2 weeks.

HAITIAN PIKLIZ

MAKES APPROXIMATELY 1 ½ CUPS
(340 ML)

4 ½ ounces (120 g) white cabbage
1 medium carrot (50 g)
1 large shallot
3 Scotch bonnet peppers
¼ teaspoon of brown cane sugar
10 cloves
8 allspice berries
½ cup (100 ml) apple cider vinegar
salt and freshly ground black pepper

YOU'LL ALSO NEED
a mandoline
a sterilized jar of approximately
1 ½ cup (350 ml) capacity (see p. 200)

PICKLED BIRAMBI AND RED ONION

MAKES APPROXIMATELY 1 ½ CUPS
(340 ML)

1 tablespoon plus 2 teaspoons of apple
cider vinegar

4 tablespoons of brown cane sugar

¾ teaspoon of salt

1 red onion

7 ounces (200 g) of birambi (available
frozen), thawed

6 allspice berries

2 bay leaves

½ Scotch bonnet pepper

YOU'LL ALSO NEED

a sterilized jar of approximately
1 ½ cup (340 ml) capacity (see p. 200)

I first encountered this pickle in a Caribbean food store in the Dapper neighborhood of Amsterdam: I saw the plastic bags filled with pink liquid with slices of red onion and oblong fruits floating in it and wanted to taste it immediately—I had a vague memory of something similar in Grenada. The birambi was surprisingly crunchy and juicy and had perfectly absorbed the flavor of the juice.

Sweet and sour: this pickle is delicious with just about everything, or on its own as a snack, for pickle enthusiasts like myself. Birambi isn't very easy to find. Look in the freezer of Asian markets—if you're lucky, you might even find them fresh. If that's the case, take them right away and make a double batch of this recipe. Trust me.

INSTRUCTIONS

1. Start by making the brine: Mix the vinegar with the sugar, the salt, and 1 tablespoon plus 2 teaspoons (25 ml) water in a small saucepan. Let it simmer over low heat for 5 minutes until the sugar is dissolved. Let it cool.

2. Cut the onion into 8 wedges.

3. Layer the onion, whole birambi, allspice, bay leaves, and Scotch bonnet in the jar. Pour the brine over it. Store in the refrigerator. The pickle will be ready after 1 month, and it can be stored for an additional 3 months. Enjoy these exciting flavors!

TRINI
CHOW CHOW

MAKES APPROXIMATELY 4 ½ POUNDS

1 red bell pepper

1 orange pepper

2 mini cucumbers

1 medium onion

1 carrot

1 zucchini

6 Madame Jeanette chili peppers

Half a cauliflower (about 10.5 ounces
or 300 grams)

1 chayote

3 tablespoons of salt

2 ½ cups (600 ml) white wine vinegar

4 tablespoons of cornstarch

1 tablespoon of ground turmeric

1 tablespoon of Caribbean curry powder
(see p. 50)

2 tablespoons of brown cane sugar

10 allspice berries

2 tablespoons of mustard powder

3 bay leaves

15 cloves

YOU'LL ALSO NEED
6 sterilized jars of approximately 1 ½ cup
(340 ml) capacity (see p. 200)

My father's cousin Earl's Trini chow chow is renowned. This addictive pickle was so popular that he began selling jars of it. He always made it so fiery and tart that upon opening a jar, my mouth would instantly water, my nose would tingle, and tears would fill my eyes. The vegetables are pickled in salt and added raw to the jar, so they retain their bite. I use cho cho, which you can find as chayote in most Asian markets. It's super crunchy, perfect for this pickle. If you can't find chayote, you can simply omit it.

This spicy and tangy pickle is delicious on crackers with cheese—a family favorite—on your favorite tacos, or really anything you're craving at the moment. Make a large batch and consider gifting some jars.

INSTRUCTIONS

1. Dice all the vegetables into tiny cubes. Put them in a large bowl and add enough water to cover. Add the salt; the water should be as salty as seawater. Cover and refrigerate overnight.

2. Take a large deep pan and add the vinegar. In a small bowl, mix 2 tablespoons of vinegar with the cornstarch. Add this to the pan, along with the turmeric, Caribbean curry powder, sugar, allspice, mustard powder, bay leaves, and cloves. Whisk until it reaches the consistency of a relish. Remove the allspice, bay leaves, and cloves.

3. Take the vegetables out of the refrigerator. Drain them well and add them to the pan. Warm for 5 minutes.

4. Divide the chow chow among sterilized jars and allow to cool. Store in the refrigerator for up to 3 months.

This chutney is the perfect accompaniment to Trini doubles (see p. 153). Well, actually, it goes with just about any dish..

INSTRUCTIONS

Grate the cucumber and garlic over a bowl. Finely chop the rawit or bird's eye chili and add. Mix in the vinegar and sugar and season with salt and pepper.

CUCUMBER CHUTNEY

MAKES 1 SERVING

1 mini cucumber

1 garlic clove

½ a rawit (or chili pepper)

¾ teaspoon of apple cider vinegar

½ teaspoon of granulated sugar

salt and freshly ground black pepper

I have vivid memories of the ultra-fresh tamarind pods, straight from the tamarind tree in my grandmother's backyard in Grenada. Once I tasted one of the sour-and-sweet fruits, I couldn't tear myself away from the tree: for hours with puckered lips from the tang of the fruit, I'd knock the pods out of the tree. This city child had never tasted anything like it. There's something special about tamarind. Not only the unique taste, but also the fact that you have to break open the pods and navigate your tongue around the seeds. This sauce is sweeter than the fruit itself. Perfect with Indian-inspired Caribbean dishes, such as aloo pies (see p. 68) and Trini doubles (see p. 153).

INSTRUCTIONS

1. In a small pot, bring 2 cups (500 ml) of water to a boil. Add the tamarind and stir until it is dissolved. Then add the jaggery, ginger, cayenne, and salt. Allow it to simmer gently for 20 minutes, until the sauce clings to a spoon. Let it cool.

2. Store the sauce in a sterilized jar in the refrigerator for up to 2 months.

TAMARIND SAUCE

MAKES APPROXIMATELY 1 ½ CUPS (340 ML)

3 tablespoons of tamarind paste

1 cup (200 grams) jaggery (see p. 46) or brown cane sugar

1 teaspoon of salt

1 teaspoon of ground ginger

1 teaspoon of cayenne pepper

YOU'LL ALSO NEED

1 sterilized jar of approximately 1 ½ cup (340 ml) capacity (see p. 200)

"Bajan" is another way to say Barbadian—something or someone from Barbados. This hot pepper sauce is used frequently and copiously in the island. The ingredient that distinguishes Bajan hot pepper sauce from other Caribbean hot sauces is mustard powder, which gives it a distinctive yellow color and a sharp taste. I also add a bit of orange zest for a slight sweet hint.

INSTRUCTIONS

1. Put the onion and Scotch bonnets in a blender and pulse to a coarse consistency. Pour the mixture into a large saucepan and add the turmeric, mustard powder, sugar, vinegar, salt, and ½ cup (120 ml) of water.

2. Heat on low and let it simmer for 20 minutes. Turn off the heat and add the orange zest.

3. Transfer to a sterilized jar and store for up to 1 month in the refrigerator.

BAJAN HOT PEPPER SAUCE

MAKES APPROXIMATELY 1 ½ CUPS
(340 ML)

1 onion
2 Scotch bonnet peppers
1 tablespoon ground turmeric
1 ½ tablespoons of mustard powder
1 ½ tablespoons of brown cane sugar
½ cup (120 ml) apple cider vinegar
1 teaspoon of salt
grated zest of 1 organic orange

YOU'LL ALSO NEED
1 sterilized jar of approximately 1 ½ cup
(340 ml) capacity (see p. 200)

Technically speaking, this salsa is not strictly Caribbean, but more inspired by South American flavors. I'm not stringent about this distinction, as it's important to remember that the original inhabitants of the Caribbean came from South America—some even from North America. Hence, there are many similarities between the two regions.

Peanuts originally come from South America, and you frequently see them in the Caribbean, especially in candies and sweet drinks. Here, I combined them with various dried chilies. It's a fantastic condiment to always have in your refrigerator: use it as a flavor enhancer in a dish or as a topping, as a marinade for chicken wings, or mix with coconut milk for a quick and delicious sauce.

Purchase the dried peppers at a well-stocked tropical store or online, for instance, at Tjin's.

INSTRUCTIONS

1. Put all the dried peppers in a bowl and pour boiling water over them so they are fully submerged. Let them soak for 10 minutes. Remove them from the water and put them in a food processor.

2. In the meantime, gently heat the unpeeled garlic cloves and olive oil in a small saucepan over low heat. Allow them to confit for 20 minutes. Turn off the heat and let the oil cool.

3. Toast the peanuts in a dry pan and chop them roughly. Add them to the chilies in the food processor.

4. Squeeze the confit garlic cloves out of their skins and add them to the food processor, along with 5 tablespoons (74 ml) of the garlic oil, the sugar, the juice and zest of the lime, thyme leaves, and salt and pepper to taste. Pulse about 6 times until you reach a relatively coarse consistency. Taste and add more salt if needed.

5. Transfer the salsa to a sterilized jar and store it for up to 3 weeks in the refrigerator.

CHILI-PEANUT-LIME SALSA

MAKES APPROXIMATELY 1 ½ CUPS
(340 ML)

2 dried guajillo chilies
1 dried chipotle
1 dried cascabel
2 dried ancho chilies
1 dried mulato
2 unpeeled cloves of garlic
1 cup (200 ml) olive oil
3 ounces (80 grams) of unsalted peanuts
2 tablespoons of granulated sugar
grated zest and juice of 1 organic lime
5 sprigs of thyme, leaves stripped
salt and freshly ground black pepper

YOU'LL ALSO NEED
1 sterilized jar of approximately 1 ½ CUPS
(340 ml) capacity (see p. 200).

TRINI CHOW

MAKES 2-3 SERVINGS

1 green mango
1 clove of garlic
⅛ teaspoon of finely chopped ginger
2 tablespoons of roughly chopped cilantro
½ a rawit (or chili pepper)
juice of 1 ½ limes
½ teaspoon of granulated sugar
salt to taste

This dish uses green, unripe mangos, a common ingredient in many Asian cuisines. The recipe originates from the Indian community of Trinidad, where it is highly cherished. It's especially popular for breakfast alongside bakkeljauw fritters or baigan choka and roti—but is just as delightful as a salad, atop a stew, burger, or sandwich. It's supremely easy to prepare and packed full of flavor.

INSTRUCTIONS

1. Peel the mango and slice the flesh away from the pit. Cut into thin strips.

2. Finely chop the garlic, ginger, cilantro, and rawit chili, and mix in a bowl with the lime juice, sugar, and mango. Season generously with salt.

3. Trini chow can be stored in the refrigerator for a few days if kept in an airtight container.

PINEAPPLE CHILI SAUCE

MAKES APPROXIMATELY 1 ½ CUPS (340 ML)

1 pineapple
1 shallot
2 cloves of garlic
1 Madame Jeanette chili pepper
1 green cardamom pod
1 tablespoon of apple cider vinegar
1 teaspoon of salt

ADDITIONAL NEEDS
a mortar and pestle
a sterilized jar of about 1 ½ cups (340 ml)
volume (refer to p. 200)

For me, pineapple is the common thread of the Caribbean: it is the quintessential symbol of tropical life. Its natural sweetness and flavor are so perfect, one might think there's no need for embellishment—unless you encounter a recipe like this chili sauce. Sweet, fruity, fragrant, and just when you believe your palate is already in a state of bliss, you get an added kick from the chili pepper. So, if you're a fan of a thrilling roller-coaster ride for your taste buds, I'd suggest making a few jars of this sauce, ensuring you never run out.

INSTRUCTIONS

1. Peel the pineapple and remove the tough core (you can use this for tepache as mentioned on p. 232). Cut the pineapple into large pieces and put them into a blender, along with the shallot, garlic, and Madame Jeanette chili pepper.

2. Blend until smooth and pour into a medium-sized saucepan.

3. Bruise the cardamom pod in a mortar and pestle and grind the seeds to a fine powder. Add this to the sauce along with the vinegar, and let it simmer on low heat for 30 minutes.

4. Add the salt toward the end.

5. Pour the sauce into a sterilized jar and store for up to 3 weeks in the refrigerator.

TOMATO SAUCE WITH DRIED SHRIMP

MAKES APPROXIMATELY 1 ½ CUPS
(340 ML)

2 cloves of garlic

~ 1-inch piece (¾ ounce or 20 grams)
of ginger, peeled

~ 1 teaspoon (3 grams) of dried shrimp

1 medium shallot

2 tablespoons of palm oil

~ 1 Scotch bonnet pepper (8 grams)

6 sprigs of thyme, leaves picked

7 ounces (200 grams) of tomatoes

½ tablespoon of tomato paste

1 teaspoon of apple cider vinegar

½ teaspoon of brown sugar

salt and freshly ground black pepper

YOU'LL ALSO NEED

a mortar and pestle

a sterilized jar of about 1½ cups (340 ml)
volume (refer to p. 200)

As I wrote at the beginning of this book, the Caribbean cuisine is a great melting pot of food cultures and shows many similarities with cuisines from the other side of the Atlantic Ocean. In many African cultures, they use dried, smoked, and/or salted fish in stews, soups, and sauces to deepen the flavor. Although you will often find salted fish in Caribbean dishes, dried and smoked fish are less common. Still, my father told me that his Mammy (the woman who took care of him when his parents worked in London) put smoked herring in the stews. A grand treat, since the fish was imported from Europe. This recipe includes dried shrimp, available in many African shops. Or use shrimp paste, which gives the same deep flavor.

INSTRUCTIONS

1. Chop the garlic and ginger finely and grind in a mortar and pestle into a smooth paste. Add the shrimp and grind them finely.

2. Chop the shallot finely and gently fry in the palm oil until translucent. Finely chop the Scotch bonnet and add it to the shallot, along with the garlic-ginger paste and thyme leaves. Roughly chop the tomatoes and add them to the pan, along with the tomato paste, apple cider vinegar, sugar, and salt and pepper to taste. Let it simmer gently until you have a thick sauce, in about 30 minutes. Taste and add generous salt.

3. Serve in a dip bowl or spoon into a sterilized jar and store for up to 5 days in the refrigerator. It is a fantastic dip for the akkras on page 80 or any other snacks.

SPICY MAYO

MAKES APPROXIMATELY ⅓ CUP (75 ML)

2 tablespoons Encona original
hot pepper sauce

3 tablespoons Hellmann's mayonnaise

This is hardly a recipe, more a clever combination of condiments. Condiments that are made to be eaten together, if you ask me. I love this spicy mayonnaise on sandwiches (with tuna, for example), with fries, with a steak, or on a burger. It's also delicious with the fried chicken (see p. 165) or okra fries (see p. 85). It's incredibly versatile, so get started. .

INSTRUCTIONS

Mix the chili sauce with the mayonnaise in a bowl.

This coconut-lime yogurt is a refreshing accompaniment to spicy curries, or as a base to serve grilled vegetables. I also always eat it with Trini doubles (see p. 153).

INSTRUCTIONS

In a bowl, mix the yogurt with the lime zest and season with salt.

COCONUT-LIME YOGURT

MAKES APPROXIMATELY ½ CUP (100 ML)

6 ½ tablespoons of coconut yogurt
(Abbott Kinney's)
grated zest of 1 organic lime
salt to taste

Papayas are super sweet tropical fruits that, when they begin to overripe, develop a sort of fermented sweetness. It's the perfect moment to make a chili sauce out of it. This sauce pairs well with the fish dishes from this book.

INSTRUCTIONS

1. Put the papaya, shallots, ginger, garlic, thyme leaves, Scotch bonnet pepper, and vinegar into a blender and blend until smooth. Scoop the mixture into a thick-bottomed pan and add the cinnamon, bay leaves, allspice berries, sugar, and salt. Allow it to simmer gently for about 30 minutes.

2. Taste to see if you want to add more salt. Stir in the butter and let it cool. Remove the cinnamon stick, bay leaves, and allspice berries from the sauce. Pour the sauce into a sterilized jar and store in the refrigerator for up to 3 weeks.

PAPAYA CHILI SAUCE

MAKES APPROXIMATELY 1 ½ CUPS (240 ML)

1 ripe papaya, peeled and seeds removed
(about 1 pound or 500 grams)
2 shallots
2 tablespoons of peeled and finely grated ginger
3 cloves of garlic
5 sprigs of thyme leaves
1 Scotch bonnet pepper
¼ cup (50 ml) apple cider vinegar
1 cinnamon stick
3 bay leaves
5 allspice berries
2 tablespoons of brown sugar
1 teaspoon of salt
1 tablespoon of salted butter

YOU'LL ALSO NEED
a sterilized jar of about 1 ½ cups (340 ml)
volume (refer to p. 200)

This pepper sauce is very addictive; you'll want to eat it on everything. I used yellow tomatoes because it was summer, and tomatoes of all colors and sizes were abundant, but you can also use red ones. Remember that in something as simple as tomato pepper sauce, the quality of the tomatoes makes a significant difference to the final taste. So look for delicious tomatoes, in season. The same goes for palm oil: you can find good quality in organic stores.

INSTRUCTIONS

Preheat the oven to 430°F (220°C). Place the tomatoes in a baking dish and mix in the olive oil. Bake for 10 minutes.

TOMATO PEPPER SAUCE

MAKES APPROXIMATELY 1 ½ CUPS
(340 ML)

3 medium tomatoes (I used yellow tomatoes, but red ones will also work)
1 tablespoon olive oil
1 medium onion
2 cloves of garlic
~ 2 teaspoons of ginger, peeled (10 grams)
2 yellow Scotch bonnet peppers
2 Maggi cubes or 1 vegetable bouillon cube
¾ teaspoon granulated sugar
¾ teaspoon apple cider vinegar
2 tablespoons plus ½ teaspoon of unrefined palm oil
Salt and freshly ground black pepper

YOU'LL ALSO NEED
a sterilized jar with approximately 1 ½ cups (340 ml) capacity (see p. 200)

In South and Central American cultures, one can find many refreshing beverages often referred to as agua fresca. These drinks are typically made with fruit, or flowers, or seeds, and a touch of sugar. Similar thirst-quenchers can also be found on the Caribbean islands, usually enriched with the creamy sweetness of condensed milk.

These drinks were a staple at family meals during my childhood, or we would pick them up from a Caribbean food store in London's Brixton. Sometimes, on Sundays, my father would whip up a Guinness punch—a concoction that remains my favorite to this day. As a child, I was allowed a tiny taste, and since I thought it contained no alcohol, I would always attempt to return for a second round. This delectable blend of Irish stout and Caribbean spices is a prime example of the mixed cultures that shape the Caribbean.

So, whether you're looking for beverages that invigorate your taste buds on a hot summer day or transport you to the tropics on a dreary winter day, you'll find them here. Serve them with plenty of ice and a splash of rum, if you're so inclined.

DRINKS

PINEAPPLES

The pineapple is the quintessential symbol of the Caribbean and the epitome of the exotic. Its flamboyant leaves reminiscent of a palm tree and prickly exterior shield a heart of the sweetest, most delightful fruit. Though native to South America and cultivated by the Mayans and Aztecs, Christopher Columbus first tasted pineapple in Guadeloupe, taking several back to Spain. Only one survived the journey, but King Ferdinand II was immediately smitten, declaring its flavor superior to all other fruits. The pineapple, which in Spanish was called "piña" due to its resemblance to a pinecone, soon became known as "pineapple" in English. The name "ananas," now used in many languages, originates from Tupi, the language of the indigenous people of modern-day Brazil. Interestingly, in Brazil, the pineapple is called "abacaxi," which in Tupi means "fruit with a pleasant aroma."

In sixteenth-century Europe, the pineapple was so rare and extraordinary that it became a status symbol. The elite decorated their palaces with sculptures and images of the fruit, and those looking to impress their guests would rent a pineapple as a centerpiece for a party. Not for eating—far too expensive—but for admiring all evening.

TEPACHE

MAKES 8 GLASSES

1 ripe pineapple (you will use only the peel and core)
1 cup (130 grams) jaggery or brown cane sugar
2 cinnamon sticks
2 cloves
¼ of a Scotch bonnet pepper

YOU'LL ALSO NEED
1 sterilized jar, approximately 1 quart (1 liter) in capacity (see p. 200)
rubber band
ice cubes (optional)

* Use the remaining pineapple flesh for the pineapple-chili sauce (see p. 218).

When I was brainstorming a corresponding drink for a Code Noir dinner, I learned about the indigenous tribes in the Caribbean who made a fermented drink from sweet potatoes. It seemed logical, given the abundance of the tuber in the area. However, my limited experience with fermentation—I had only dabbled in kombucha and something akin to vinegar—made me wary of experimenting. Fortunately, the chef at Mediamatic, an art and technology center in Amsterdam where the dinner was to take place, suggested making tepache, a fermented beverage from pineapple peel. The Aztecs in pre-Columbian Mexico originally used corn to make the drink, as "tepiātl" translates to "drink of corn."

The drink was such a success at the dinner that I've been regularly making batches ever since, and even assembling ingredient packages for friends—it's incredibly easy to make. Just like with kombucha, you can add various flavor enhancers at the end. I opted for Scotch bonnet, but ginger, lavender, or thyme are also great options.

Tepache is in line with the no-waste trend, as it uses only the peel and the hard core of the pineapple. It's refreshing, highly flavorful, and packed with excellent probiotics from the fermentation.

INSTRUCTIONS

1. To start, peel the pineapple and cut away the flesh around the hard core. Set the peel and core aside.

2. In a pot, bring 1 quart (1 liter) of water and the jaggery to a boil. Turn off the heat once the sugar is dissolved and allow it to cool to room temperature.

3. Place the pineapple peel and core, the sugar water, the cinnamon, and the cloves in the sterilized jar. Cover with a tea towel and secure with a rubber band. Let it sit for 2 days in a cool, dark place, such as the refrigerator.

4. Remove the pineapple and spices from the drink. Add the Scotch bonnet (or use less for a less spicy flavor). Place in the refrigerator to fully chill. Serve as is, or with ice cubes.

5. If the tepache is not consumed in one sitting, remove the pepper from the pitcher before returning it to the refrigerator. Otherwise, the tepache will become too spicy to drink. Store the drink for up to one month in the refrigerator.

NUTMEG

Nutmeg holds an essential place in both sweet and savory dishes across the Caribbean, enhancing everything from curries, stews, and jerk recipes to macaroni and cheese and sweet potato pies. The spice itself is the nut, enveloped by a vibrant red layer called mace.

For centuries, nutmeg only grew in the Moluccas, in the eastern part of what is now Indonesia. However, it was deeply adored by elites far beyond these islands for its unique taste, scarcity, and its reputed hallucinogenic properties.

The history of this spice is a tragic one, particularly in the Banda Islands, which for a long time were the sole source of nutmeg and mace. The Dutch trading company, VOC (Vereenigde Oostindische Compagnie, 1602-1799), was determined to monopolize this rare commodity. To this end, Governor-General Jan

Pieterszoon Coen orchestrated the massacre of almost the entire population of these islands in 1621. The enormous profits nutmeg brought explains why, in 1667, the Republic of the Seven United Netherlands agreed to exchange the insignificant island of Manhattan in New Amsterdam with the British for the small island of Pulau Run, one of the Banda Islands where nutmeg grew aplenty.

Nutmeg would eventually give one Caribbean island its moniker as the "Island of Spice." In the latter half of the nineteenth century, the British—having finally managed to smuggle nutmeg out of the Moluccas— introduced the plant to Sri Lanka and the West Indies. Grenada, in particular, proved to have the perfect climate for this spice. Today, this country has become the second-largest producer after Indonesia, with the prominent depiction of a nutmeg on Grenada's flag testifying to its importance.

GUINNESS PUNCH

A few years back, I was instructing at a summer school on the culinary history of the Caribbean. During the interactive workshop, students devised food rituals, summoned significant food memories, and crafted a Caribbean cocktail. They chose to make a Guinness Punch—a favorite on several British-colonized islands. This mixture of strong stout beer, creamy, sweet condensed milk, and a hint of cinnamon and nutmeg is a delightful fusion of flavors.

Guinness was known to me through both sides of my family. The Irish connection was apparent since Guinness was founded in Dublin, but why was it also known from the Caribbean side? As it turns out, in the seventeenth century, the Irish were engaged as contract laborers on plantations in the Caribbean. Due to their substantial presence in the area, Guinness decided to export beer there—with more alcohol and hops, ensuring it stayed good during the transatlantic journey. When I learned this, I felt a strong sense of connection: the unlikely merging of two clashing cultures had given rise to something beautiful and tasty—and no, I'm not referring to myself!

INSTRUCTIONS

Place all ingredients, except the ice cubes, into a blender and pulse several times. Serve in glasses with ice cubes and a sprinkle of freshly grated nutmeg on top.

Mangoes—who doesn't love them? I adore all kinds, or at least those I've tasted. There are reportedly 355 varieties sold, and over five hundred exist. I have vivid memories of plucking mangoes as a child in my aunt's garden. I plucked and ate, the juice running down my face: a fitting reward for hard work.

Blending mango with yogurt and cardamom makes it even more delicious and especially refreshing. Alphonso mangoes are buttery and extra sweet—I regard them as the ultimate mango. Mango lassi isn't typically Caribbean, but the significant Indian diaspora on the islands means this recipe could not be missing. It's a tribute to all people with Indian and Caribbean roots and to the fantastic fruit, the mango.

INSTRUCTIONS

1. Place the mango pulp and Greek yogurt in a blender. Bruise the black and green cardamom pods in a mortar and grind the seeds into fine powder. Add them, along with the salt, to the mango and blend until smooth.

2. Serve in glasses with plenty of ice.

GUINNESS PUNCH

MAKES 4-5 GLASSES

1 bottle (500 ml or roughly 2 cups) of Guinness West Indies Porter
1 cup (250 ml) (oat) milk
½ cup (120 ml) of condensed milk
⅛ teaspoon ground cinnamon
⅛ teaspoon freshly grated nutmeg, plus extra
¼ teaspoon vanilla extract
2 tablespoons overproof rum (high-alcohol rum; optional)
ice cubes, to serve

MANGO LASSI

MAKES 4 GLASSES

2 pounds (850 grams) of Alphonso mangoes (weighed without peel and pit), cut into pieces—or buy canned pulp at Indian stores or online.
1 ½ cups (350 grams) of Greek yogurt
6 black cardamom pods
2 green cardamom pods
a pinch of Maldon salt or coarse sea salt
ice cubes, to serve

YOU'LL ALSO NEED
a mortar and pestle

HIBISCUS SYRUP

MAKES 10 GLASSES

3-4 inch piece of ginger (65 grams)
~ 2 cups (150 grams) of dried hibiscus
(use fresh if you can find it)
6 allspice berries
2 cinnamon sticks
2 ¼ cups (450 grams) of cane sugar
sparkling water or Prosecco, for serving
ice cubes, for serving

YOU'LL ALSO NEED

a skimmer
a sterilized 2-liter (about 2-quart) bottle
(see p. 200)

Growing up, I was enamored with this deep ruby-red drink. Traditionally served around Christmas, I remember my parents soaking the hibiscus a month before the holiday for a flavor-packed result. The flower has many names, such as flor de Jamaica, roselle, empire tea, carcade, and sorrel—which in the Caribbean means hibiscus, not sourgrass. The flower originates from West Africa, and it's said that enslaved Africans, who used it for medicinal and culinary purposes, brought it across the ocean. Hibiscus has a unique flavor: floral, tart, with a good amount of acidity. It pairs perfectly with spices and sugar. Mix with sparkling water or Prosecco.

INSTRUCTIONS

1. Pour 2 liters (about 8 ½ cups) of water into a pot and bring it to a boil. Roughly chop the ginger (no need to peel) and add it to the pot along with the hibiscus, allspice, cinnamon, and cane sugar. Let it cook for 20 minutes. Remove the pot from the heat and let it cool. Leave to infuse overnight in a cool place.

2. Use a skimmer to remove the hibiscus and spices from the pot. Pour the syrup into a sterilized bottle and store in the refrigerator until use. The syrup will keep for a month.

3. Serve 4 tablespoons of syrup diluted with sparkling water and plenty of ice, or, for an adult version, with Prosecco.

LIMEADE SYRUP

I received this recipe from a friend who bought a refreshing cinnamon drink from a street vendor during a trip through Guatemala. Cinnamon water is not traditionally Caribbean, but since Grenada is known as the Island of Spice and a lot of Ceylon cinnamon grows there, it should not be missing in this book.

INSTRUCTIONS

1. Put 2 liters (about 8 ½ cups) of water, the cinnamon sticks, and cane sugar in a pot and let it simmer gently for 20 minutes. Remove from the heat and let it cool completely. Strain the cinnamon water into a pitcher, discarding the cinnamon sticks.

2. Pour the drink into a sterilized bottle and store it for up to a week in the refrigerator.

3. Serve the cinnamon water with plenty of ice and a slice of lime.

CINNAMON WATER

MAKES ABOUT 8 GLASSES

10 (approximately 3-inch) cinnamon sticks
~ ⅔ cup (130 grams) of cane sugar
ice cubes, for serving
1 lime, sliced

YOU'LL ALSO NEED
a sterilized 2-liter (about 2-quart) bottle (see p. 200)

Limeade syrup is a remix of the familiar lemonade: use lime zest and lime juice instead of lemon. It's incredibly tangy, citrusy, and refreshing. Serve with lots of ice, and if you want to be a bit cheeky, a dash of rum.

INSTRUCTIONS

1. Heat the sugar, lime juice, and zest with ˌ 1 cup (200 milliliters) of water in a small saucepan over low heat. Let it simmer gently for 30 minutes or until the mixture has the consistency of syrup.

2. Let it cool. Pour into a pitcher with sparkling water to taste and lots of ice.

LIMEADE SYRUP

MAKES 1 LARGE PITCHER

½ cup (100 grams) of sugar
grated zest and juice of 4 organic limes
sparkling water, for serving
ice cubes, for serving

GINGER BEER SYRUP

Disclaimer: This ginger syrup is SPICY. But given the seemingly endless list of ginger's health benefits, I'd willingly endure a fiery mouth. Oh, and it's delicious, too, did I mention that? Ginger beer originated from colonial trade routes: Asian ginger and Caribbean sugar came together in this low-alcohol beverage. This syrup is not fermented, so it contains no alcohol. Mix with still or sparkling water, or take a straight shot to ward off a cold or impending flu.

INSTRUCTIONS

1. Chop the ginger roughly and blend with about 2 cups (500 ml) of water until smooth. Pour into a pan and warm the mixture with the sugar, allspice, and pepper on medium heat. Let it simmer on low heat for 30 minutes or until the sugar has dissolved.

2. Turn off the heat and let it steep with the lid on the pot for several hours, or better yet, overnight at room temperature. This will give you a lightly fermented drink.

3. Add the lime juice. Strain the mixture into a pitcher and pour it into a sterilized bottle.

4. Serve with sparkling water and ice.

5. Store the syrup for up to 3 months in the refrigerator.

GINGER BEER SYRUP

MAKES ABOUT 1 1/4 CUPS (300 ML)

4 ¼ ounces (120 grams) of ginger, peeled
½ cup (100 grams) of brown cane sugar
4 allspice berries
4 black peppercorns
juice of 2 limes
seltzer water, to serve
ice cubes, to serve

YOU'LL ALSO NEED
a sterilized bottle with a capacity of about 1 ½ cups (340 ml) (see p. 200)

Even though peanuts are plentiful and originally come from South America, they surprisingly feature little in Caribbean cuisine. They're primarily used in sweets or sweet drinks, like in this peanut punch. Velvety smooth, wonderfully sweet, with a hint of spices.

INSTRUCTIONS

Combine all ingredients (including the 10 ice cubes) with ¾ cup plus 2 tablespoons (200 ml) of water in a blender and mix for 5 minutes. Serve with extra ice.

PEANUT PUNCH

MAKES 6-7 GLASSES

9 tablespoons smooth peanut butter
¾ cup plus 2 tablespoons (200 ml) coconut milk
3 tablespoons condensed milk
⅛ teaspoon freshly grated cinnamon stick
a pinch (¼ teaspoon) of freshly grated nutmeg
10 ice cubes, plus extra

BIBLIOGRAPHY

Candice Goucher, *Congotay! Congotay!:
A Global History of Caribbean Foo*d, 2014.

Jessica B. Harris, *Iron Pots and Wooden Spoons—Africa's Gifts
to New World Cooking*, 1999.

Jessica B. Harris, *Sky Juice and Flying Fish:
Traditional Caribbean Cooking*, 1991.

Michelle & Suzanne Rousseau, *Provisions:
The Roots of Caribbean Cooking*, 2018.

Rui Da Silva, *A Quick Ting on: Plantain*, 2022.

Raymond Sokolov, *Why We Eat What We Eat*, 1991.

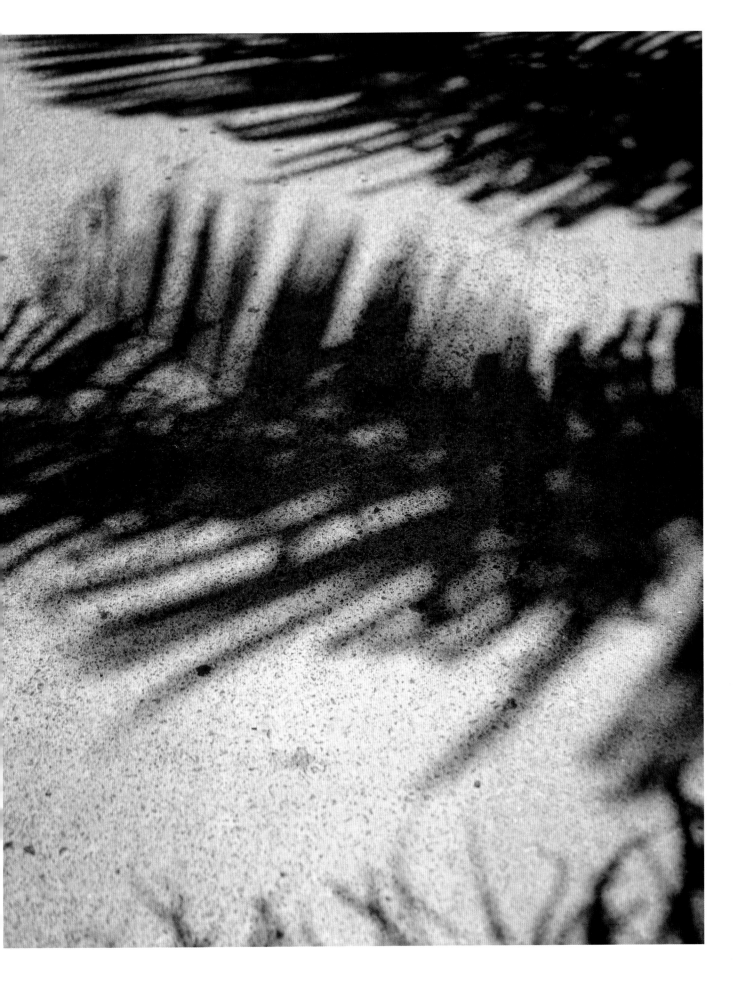

INDEX

SALTED FISH

Saltfish and ackee 136
Saltfish fritters 73
Saltfish in coconut milk with green papaya 139
Saltfish souse and bakes 133

SALTED MEAT

Pepperpot soup with spinners 168

SALTFISH AND ACKEE 136

SALTFISH FRITTERS 73

SALTFISH IN COCONUT MILK WITH GREEN PAPAYA 139

SALTFISH SOUSE AND BAKES 133

SCALLION

Cornbread 158
Corn fritters 85
Corn ribs with scallion-jalapeño butter 71
Curry goat 148
Green seasoning 51
Jerk marinade 57
Pepperpot soup with spinners 168
Pickapeppa 58
Rice and peas 58
Saltfish and ackee 136
Saltfish fritters 73
Saltfish souse and bakes 133
Sweet potato patties in callaloo coconut sauce 112

SCALLION-JALAPEÑO BUTTER

Corn ribs with scallion-jalapeño butter 71
Cornbread 158

SEA BASS

Ceviche 124

SEA BREAM

Fish with mojo 135

SHALLOT

Akkras (black-eyed pea fritters) 80
Baigan choka with coconut tun (roasted eggplant and coconut polenta) 104
Coconut dahl 98
Haitian pikliz 205
Jerk marinade 57
Papaya chili sauce 223
Pepperpot soup with spinners 168
Pineapple chili sauce 218
Tomato sauce with dried shrimp 222

SHIITAKE MUSHROOM

Stewed peas with spinners 101

SHRIMP

Peppered shrimp 74
Tomato sauce with dried shrimp 222

SPICY MAYO 222

STEWED PEAS WITH SPINNERS 101

SWEET POTATO

Brown butter sweet potato pudding 187
Cassava bread with lima beans and corn relish 66
Conrad's chicken curry 145
Pepperpot soup with spinners 168
Sweet potato gratin with ginger cream 173
Sweet potato patties in callaloo coconut sauce 112

SWEET POTATO GRATIN WITH GINGER CREAM 173

SWEET POTATO LEAF

Pepperpot soup with spinners 168
Red snapper with cassava purée, callaloo coconut sauce, and cassava chips 121
Saltfish in coconut milk with green papaya 139
Sweet potato patties in callaloo coconut sauce 112

SWEET POTATO PATTIES IN CALLALOO COCONUT SAUCE 112

TAMARIND PASTE

Tamarind sauce 213

TAMARIND SAUCE 213

TEPACHE 232

THYME

Akkras (black-eyed pea fritters) 80
Cassava bread with lima beans and corn relish 66
Chili-peanut-lime salsa 217
Conrad's chicken curry 145
Cornbread 158
Corn fritters 85
Corn ribs with scallion-jalapeño butter 71
Curry goat 148
Escovitch fish 122
Green seasoning 51
Jerk marinade 57
Papaya chili sauce 223
Pasteles 77
Pepperpot soup with spinners 168
Pepperpot stew 154
Pickapeppa sauce 58
Rice and peas 58
Rice and peas arancini 89
Saltfish and ackee 136
Saltfish fritters 73
Stewed peas with spinners 101
Sweet potato gratin with ginger cream 173
Sweet potato patties in callaloo coconut sauce 112
Thyme oil 60
Tomato sauce with dried shrimp 222

THYME OIL 60

Red snapper with cassava purée, callaloo coconut sauce, and cassava chips 121

TOMATOES

Baigan choka with coconut tun (roasted eggplant and coconut polenta) 104
Pickapeppa sauce 58
Roasted mojo pork shoulder 163
Saltfish and ackee 136
Saltfish souse and bakes 133
Tomato pepper sauce 225
Tomato sauce with dried shrimp 222

ACKNOWLEDGMENTS

I want to take this moment to thank all the people who have made this book possible. A personal cookbook has always been a dream of mine, and Code Noir is thus a labor of immense love. It allowed me to draw upon countless cherished memories of my family, brimming with joy and celebration, all the while making me reflect on how Caribbean cuisines have evolved. It is a poignant reminder that some culinary traditions are born from oppression.

I would like to express my deep gratitude and praises to my family: my seemingly infinite list of aunts, uncles, cousins, grandparents, and most importantly, my father, Conrad Lewis, and mother, Sandra Lewis. They could not have anticipated that their hospitality and the joy they found in sharing their food with others would inspire me to embark on a career in the kitchen—a job I passionately love.

I owe a deep debt of thanks to my husband, Guy Lewis Wood, without whose unwavering support, patience, and unshakeable belief in me, none of this would have been possible.

I am indebted to Jill Mathon, who had steadfast faith in me from the beginning to turn my dinner concept into a book and encouraged me to write a pitch, which would become the key to getting my foot in the door. Thank you!

A heartfelt thank you to Joris Bijdendijk, my unexpected benefactor, who, as I audaciously declared, "I would like to someday make a cookbook," generously connected me with his publisher, Nijgh Cuisine.

I would like to thank my publisher, specifically Miriam Brunsveld, Nique. van den Tillaart, Sofie Langenberg, Marieke Migchelbrink, and Wouter Eertink, for believing in my book, and also for all their hard work in birthing my second child, *Code Noir*!

A special place on this list is reserved for Charlotte Kleyn: my translator and fact-checker, who not only brought order to my overall chaos and kept me sharp on deadlines but also helped me make critical decisions about the book's content.

I wish to thank all the creatives who helped bring the vision of this book to life. I asked for the very best, and fortunately for me, that's precisely what I got. Thank you, Remko Kraaijeveld, Chantal Arnts, Isabelle van der Horst, Annelies Dollekamp, Anne Lakeman, and Floyd Robinson. A big thank also to my friend and all-around creative, Matt Firth, for his help in visualizing the book cover.

Finally, I want to thank my son, Gray Lewis Wood, who inspired me to pursue what I always wanted. This book, and everything else I've achieved in my career and am yet to achieve, I owe to you.

Code Noir: Afro-Caribbean Stories and Recipes

Author
Lelani Lewis

Food Styling
Lelani Lewis

Styling
Isabelle van der Horst

Photographs
Pages 110, 111, 128, 150, 157, 210, 211, 220, and 221:
Anne Lakeman

Pages 117 and 244-245: Floyd Robinson

Pages 103, 160, and 170: Shutterstock

Page 183: Private author's archive

Endpapers: Nipanan Lifestyle
(Coconut), Bruno Nascimento (Pineapple),
Eriksson Luo (Plantain), and Elvis Amaya (Sunset)
all sourced via Unsplash

U.S. Edition Team

Publisher and Creative Director
Ilona Oppenheim

Art Director
Jefferson Quintana

Designer/Typesetter
Jefferson Quintana

Editorial Director
Lisa McGuinness

Editorial Coordinator
Jessica Faroy

Printed and bound in China by
Shenzhen Reliance Printers

ISBN: 978-1-9620980-0-7

MIX
Paper from responsible sources
FSC® C102842

Code Noir: Afro-Caribbean Stories and Recipes is printed on Forest Stewardship Council-certified paper from well-managed forests. Tra Publishing is committed to sustainability in its materials and practices.

Tra Publishing
245 NE 37th Street
Miami, FL 33137
trapublishing.com

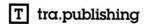

1 2 3 4 5 6 7 8 9 10